FATALLY FLAWED

THE QUEST TO BE DEEPEST!

by Verna van Schaik

Contents

Dedication

- My Mom, Denise van Schaik - for believing in me, always!

- My nieces, Michaela and Aislin - for giving me a reason to come back

- Joseph Emmanuel - there would have been no dive without him

- Gail Davidson - who was there for the whole journey and listened to all the tears

- Derek Hughes – for getting it all started, and staying to the end

- ScubaPro South Africa, in particular Rhys Couzyn and Steve Rusznyak, who provided unbelievable support and service and the best equipment ever

- Allana Barber & Kirsten Emmanuel- who arrived late, but whose support has been invaluable

- Nuno Gomes - for not taking responsibility and teaching me the basics

- Cherise Modlin and Karl Thomas - without them I would never have started to see who I could be

All the people on both my dives - without them it would never have happened

(1) The Lure of Depth

"It is the 8ᵗʰ of January 2005 and what started with enthusiasm and optimism has turned into our worst nightmare. Dave Shaw is not coming back and his buddy Don Shirley is missing. As surface marshall, I am suddenly the focus of attention. What happens now is my decision and instead of a long, boring day waiting for divers to return, I have to use everything I know about diving to world record depths to try and give the missing diver the edge that will get him out alive."

More men have landed on the moon than have dived to sub-250 meters, where there's no room for error and even less time to recover. This is the extreme edge of scuba diving; a place where you not only find out how good you are at diving but *who* you are, and this day was to go down as one of the most notorious dives in the history of deep diving. Dave Shaw had chosen to retrieve the body of a diver who had been lost for ten years. The dive would take Dave to 272 meters and cost him his life. For his buddy Don Shirley (who tried to go and help before he found himself in trouble), the price would not be quite so severe - only his balance and short term memory. This is what it took to get worldwide recognition for deep diving - the death of one man who did not believe in limits.

How did I get to be there, on that dive? Deep diving is hard to break into and getting onto a dive like Dave's even harder. Getting accepted is as much about your ability underwater as it is about how well you get on with the deep diver himself. I was there because I knew what it took to dive deep (I am officially the deepest woman in the world). I was there because they needed someone who could make the right decisions on the surface if something went wrong. *I* was their edge if anything went wrong.

Like Dave, I am an explorer, relishing the challenge of going to new places and doing things that have not been done before. We both understood that limits are choices (more liquid than fixed) and that limits change. For those of us who choose to test the limits, death is something to be accepted, not feared. Like Dave, I've made the decision to dive even if it might mean I die. I thought I knew what it took to break records, but what I hadn't understood was the *true* price of that ambition. When I am the diver, I am isolated from the true consequences and their effects on the people I might leave behind.

On that fateful day I would experience deep diving from the other side of the fence and for the first time in almost a decade inside the world of deep divers I found myself asking whether dying for a dive was really worth it. More than that, I started to wonder why risking possible death for a deep dive held such powerful attraction.

I find myself in a group of men and woman who choose to challenge not only their own limits but also those of the world, yet we have little in common other than our choices. Are we real life explorers? What drives a person to place their life on the line? Why do we want so desperately to be the deepest?

Are we fatally flawed?

Extremely Exclusive

Naming the divers who have dared to challenge depth in scuba is not hard - it is a small, select, group of men and women who dare. Deep diving is also a fairly recent phenomena, having started to gain popularity in the late 80s with Sheck Exley and his quest to find the depth limit.

Sheck's is a name that is synonymous with deep cave diving, and for many he's the founder of both. He's also one of the many divers who paid the ultimate price of being first - he died sub-280 meters whilst attempting to bottom Zacaton, a cave in

Mexico. His buddy, Jim Bowden, survived, setting (briefly) a new world record at 281 meters.

Another name that is synonymous with deep diving is that of Nuno Gomes who is the current world record holder and is not only the deepest man in the world but also the deepest man in a cave. He's a truly remarkable diver not only as a result of his depth records, but also because he's the only man to successfully dive deeper than 250 meters four times. In 1994, he set a new world record for depth with a dive to 282 meters in Boesmansgat (the third largest underwater cave in the world, located in South Africa). This deep cave record held until 2001 when John Bennett went to 308 meters in the ocean off the Philippines. Regrettably, Bennett died later doing a shallow wreck dive. His body was never recovered.

Not to be dismissed, Nuno went back, this time to dive in the ocean where he set the all time, definitive depth record with a dive to 321 meters in 2005. His 1996 dive to 282 meters in a cave remains unbroken - no one has been deeper in a cave than Nuno Gomes. The only diver who has come close is Dave Shaw, with his dive to 272 meters in Boesmansgat on a re-breather. More incredibly, no one has ever dived as many times sub-250 meters as Nuno. Most divers do one deep dive, get the record and then never go back. Nuno went back not once, but three times.

No account of the divers who dive deep can exclude Dave Shaw whose epic adventures at Boesmansgat have set him apart from those who came before. Instead of chasing a number, Dave took things one step further. He decided to explore and swim at depth, something that I doubt any open circuit diver would contemplate. Tragically, he died trying to repeat a dive to 272 meters and recover the body of a fellow diver, Deon Dreyer. The irony is that he was that he had already done the depth once before, when he discovered Deon. That dive was (and still is) a world record for depth for re-breather diving.

So far the names have all been men. It is harder to write about the women who dive deep; after all, there are only four divers who have set records for depth for women. In the 80s and 90s there were the American cave divers Mary Ellen Eckhoff and Dr Anne Kristovich, who reached 120 meters and 167 meters respectively. It took until 2001 for Italian Claudia Serpierri to reach 211 meters in the Mediterranean and in doing so set a new women's world record.

In 2001, I set a new cave world record with my dive to 186 meters at Boesmansgat. With the altitude conversion it was equivalent to 220 meters in the sea, however, to make 'the book' I needed to have one more go at it so I went back and in 2004 I broke my own record to finally get the all-time women's depth record which now stands at 221 meters.

Diving sub-200 meters does not sound hard; after all these days getting to 100-150 meters is something most divers can achieve. It is when you decide to be deepest that your odds of success start to diminish. Of the five men and four women who have chosen to be deepest, all four women are still alive but only two of the men have survived - Jim Bowden and Nuno Gomes.

But what is deep diving? When does a dive turn from shallow to deep? The scuba diving agencies have defined deep diving as any dive deeper than 40 meters. This is the point at which diving on normal air starts to cause problems (normal air is what you are breathing right now). When you dive deeper than 40 meters the nitrogen that is present in air becomes highly narcotic (a feeling not unlike having too much too drink). This is called nitrogen narcosis. Then, as you get close to 80 meters the oxygen present in normal air becomes lethal – there is simply too much of it. To avoid both narcosis and a lethal oxygen dose, divers add helium to normal air, creating a mix.

The fact that you can't use normal air to dive deeper than 100 meters safely has slowed down our quest for depth. In the early 90s the first man to get to 200 meters was so badly bent he never fully recovered. These days enough divers have been deeper than 200 meters that we have a better understanding of how the human body reacts. We know more about what can go wrong and how to manage it when it does go wrong. However, the biggest uncertainty (even now) with diving deep is the whether or not you will bend.

Bending is the one risk that no diver can truly manage. To be bent ranges from excruciating pain in your joints to severe stroke, paralysis and death. You bend if you come up from depth to quickly. In a nutshell, your body releases bubbles into your system. How badly you bend will depend on where those bubbles go. We have tables that tell us to stop so that bubbles do not form, however the tables are mathematical models which are not that good at predicting what will happen in a human body – human bodies are simply too complex. The series of stops generated from the tables is termed the decompression profile. Unfortunately following it exactly still does not guarantee that you will *not* bend. You never know on a dive if you have the decompression right, not even when you get out of the water with no incident(many divers suffer from the bends three to twelve hours after surfacing).

Bending is simply a reality of diving deep. Everyone who has dived deep has bent. It is not a question of if, but of when. No one who has dived deep for long and certainly no one who has dived deeper than 200 meters has escaped paying for that privilege physically.

Let's not kid ourselves here, diving deep is dangerous. There is a reason why life insurance companies will not insure you if you participate. Three out of the five men who have dived deeper than 250 meters are dead and the price is not restricted to the few who choose to play at the edge of reason - anyone who chooses to push their limits gets to pay.

What can happen when you choose to test your limits and dive deep?

I have sat, helpless, on the side of Boesmansgat with Nuno Gomes wrapped in an emergency blanket, white as a sheet and exhausted after his 230 meter dive. On his next dive he came out full of energy but stone deaf after a bad inner ear bend (one of the first recorded counter diffusion bends).

I was there the day fellow technical diver Erna Smith died, doing a simple 50 meter drill practicing for deep ocean dives. I sat through the search for Deon Dreyer when good friends were called upon to see if they could find his body. They never did. I saw the devastation on the dive leader's face and listened to his despair as he tried to get to grips with the death of a member of his team and friend.

I sat in awe in a packed church as the diving community sat alongside family and friends to say goodbye to Denis Harding who was yet another victim of diving deep – he died at 100 meters looking for the Coelacanth.

I have watched Joseph Emmanuel, my closest friend, not know who he was from a cerebral bend (he still claims it was a bad migraine). I was there the day that Dave Shaw died trying to recover Deon Dreyer's body at 272 meters and I was there trying to swing the odds back to Don Shirley's favour (Dave's buddy and one of South Africa's more experienced technical divers) when he suffered a catastrophic inner ear bend.

Five men, four woman and *all* you have to do is get deeper than the last one - 321 meters if you are a man, 221 meters if you are a woman … and then your name can sit alongside ours. All you have to do is want it. All you have to do is be willing pay the price.

What price would you pay for a world record? Your hearing? Your memory? Family? Relationships? Your life?

What if it wasn't just about *your* name being in a book? What price would you pay to be accepted, respected … loved?

(2) Getting Hooked on Depth

Why do we dive? Who are we? What drives us? These questions haunt me as much as the image of Dave the day they retrieved him from Boesmansgat. No one would know Dave's reasons, then again, internal introspection does not seem to be a quality that successful deep diving requires. If I wanted answers, I would have to find them for myself and that meant only one thing – understanding how I arrived with the title of deepest. Why did I choose to place my life on the line for the title?

I started diving in 1989 at Wits University (Johannesburg, South Africa). Diving back then was not the same world that divers are familiar with today, especially not when it comes to deep diving. Today (thanks in part to divers like Nuno and Sheck) technical kit can be bought off the shelf, and there are technical dive schools that supply technical diving certificates (deep diving, cave diving, decompression diving - you name it, they have it). Deep diving is accessible, safe and mostly repeatable.

Even the world of sport diving wasn't as it is today (with a PADI Dive School on every corner). Today's divers are spoilt for choice when it comes to choosing an instructor and easily rack up a list of courses starting at Open Water One.

My diving career started back when diving was in its infancy. It was the early 90s and to dive you had to join a club or find one of the two or three dive schools that did exist. Without the proliferation of dive schools that we know today, diving revolved

> ### *Sport Diving*
> What the person on the street associates with scuba diving. A sport diver dives to a max of 30 meters with a single cylinder.

around the dive clubs. These clubs were generally non-profit associations that provided training and equipment to their members with the aim to dive, not make money.

This concept of clubs with total control over their divers is important in understanding the norms that I lived within. In the early 90s, certification had little in common with what we know today. There were only two diving certificates available, an incomprehensible state of affairs when compared to the numerous courses and specialties available to a modern day diver.

Back then there was little or no need for more than two courses - certificates were not the way in which competence was ensured; that responsibility lay with the divers in the club where skill and ability were handed down using

> **Sport Diving Gear**
> - BC (Buoyancy Compensator) - jacket holding dive cylinder. By adding air to the jacket the diver is prevented from sinking below his desired depth.
> - DV (Demand Valve) - device that you breathe from.
> - SPG (Submersible Pressure Gauge) - indicates how much air is in your cylinders.
> - Dive Computer - goes on your wrist and tells you how deep you are and what your decompression is.
> - Mask and fins.

a mentorship structure. What you knew and how good you were as a diver had little to do with your certificate and everything to do with the divers who taught you.

One way of describing a typical club would be a miniature dictatorship, where one (or perhaps a couple) of divers ruled supreme. Termed Scuba Gods by the less reverent, these were men who had worked their way up the club ranks acquiring dives and perhaps skill. They were at the top of the hierarchy and they and they alone influenced what could and couldn't happen in a club.

It was in this world of strict (if not talked about) rules that I learnt to scuba dive. This informal code was especially pronounced if you wished to dive deep or in a cave. With no technical schools, you had no choice but to rely on the expertise inside your club to get you trained and onto the so-called technical dives (a technical dive is anything deeper than 30 meters, anything not on normal air and anything inside a cave or wreck).

As a diver inside a club you were totally reliant on the goodwill of the Scuba Gods and their inner circle. It didn't do to challenge the way things were if you wanted to dive. You had to fit in. Without a club how would you get the extra equipment that a deep dive needs? Where would you get support divers? Most importantly, without the expertise within the club, how did you get the information you needed that would teach you how to dive safely?

Of all the clubs I could have joined, I found myself at Wits Underwater Club, home of the soon-to-be world record holder Nuno Gomes. Fondly called WUC by its members, Wits Underwater Club made diving accessible for a poor student and because of Nuno, there was an active core group of technical divers.

As an entry-level sport diver, I wasn't really bothered by the technical guys. My passion was for the sea. I was set on being a marine biologist and wanted to know everything there was about marine life. However, the creatures I was so interested in were all out of reach from the shore. To get to them I needed to be under the water. Learning to dive was just a means to an end and I certainly had no intention of ever going deep never mind into a cave. I thought Nuno and the team he had around him were quite mad.

WUC was extremely proud of Nuno. He was (and is) one of the best divers in the world (never mind South Africa) and his quest for a world record was being played out right in front of me. What I was watching was more than an individual's ambition to be deepest. It was a rivalry. Sheck Exley had started his deep expeditions, getting deeper and deeper each year and right next to me, Nuno was doggedly pursuing the same record.

At first, this was all just an adventure that was happening around me. I was mildly curious but nothing more. I was there to dive, as much and as often as possible. Being land bound, sea diving was just too expensive. Instead, I made sure I was on every club trip to the much more accessible (and cheap) inland dive sites, specifically Wondergat.

Wondergat is a notorious sinkhole that provides not only deep open water diving, but also deep *cave* diving. With a bottom sitting between 35 and 40 meters and a cave that reaches back 60 meters it is a technically challenging and dangerous site, especially as the walls are riddled with crevices and false caverns into which the unwary diver can wander. To date, Wondergat has claimed close to 20 lives - many of those divers who were disoriented in the open hole. The essence of Wondergat and indeed technical diving is neatly summed up by the police sign, which was placed by local police divers to commemorate the many divers who lost their lives diving in Wondergat.

"You have never lived until you have almost died
and for those who fight for it,
life has a flavour the protected will never know."

Within Wondergat there are a number of pre-defined dives, each with their own difficulty grading. The back of the cave was the most difficult and had killed the most people. Then there was the Police Sign, tantalisingly just at the edge of the mouth of the cave and at 50 meters dangerous in its own right. The easiest dive of them all (but still dangerous) was the cave grid at 37 meters. Within our club these dives formed milestones in an individual's career and in order to reach each milestone there was a set of conditions that had to be fulfilled. Being able to dive the cave grid without an instructor was a major accomplishment and required a deep diving certificate in conjunction with numerous other dives to ensure that you had the right level of experience. Reaching the Police Sign was (and still is) a status symbol of note. It meant you had moved into the real technical circle. It meant you could officially dive deep.

As it was each club's responsibility to add to the training of its divers and so ensure that we didn't kill ourselves, it wasn't easy to get permission to do anything other than a 20 meter circuit (now, whilst I find Wondergat to be a fascinating place to dive, swimming round and round the walls of Wondergat at 20 meters starts to get tedious to say the least). I was getting bored. All this diving was also increasing my confidence. Maybe diving deep was not such a bad idea after all? I did not have to actually go into the cave or really, really deep – just a little bit deeper than where I was. Just to see what was there.

The Police Sign became my goal and the first step toward it was the cave grid. I was excited. The guys who were doing the deep dives always came back raving about how awesome their dives were. I was expecting to have one of the best dives of my life. Instead my first deep dive was one of my worst. I hated being deep.

> **Narcosis/Narced**
>
> The effect of nitrogen on your body when diving deeper than 30 meters.

No, I loathed it.

The dive started well. The group swam the 50 or so meters to the metal drum that signaled the start of the cave shot line. We started our descent and then simply fell through the milky water, slowly saying goodbye to the fish covered walls, until looming underneath us was the rather innocuous metal grid. Elegantly we landed on metal grid and took in the view. Not much to see really.

The cave grid does not have much of a view even when the visibility is good. It is surrounded by large boulders that block it in, making it an ideal training dive for deep dives as there is really nowhere for divers to go but the grid. From the cave shotline two additional lines moved off into the gloom, one to the police sign and one to the deep grid. Every now and then an enthusiastic barbell would wander past (not that I was really paying attention). I was narced out of my tree, totally unable to think never mind do anything and it was dark. It felt like one of those evenings when you have had way too much to drink, you get home and then spend an hour trying to switch the light on. I couldn't stand being that out of control. I was also petrified of the dark on land, never mind at 35 meters. No matter how romantic Nuno was making deep diving look, I was no longer interested. I stuck it out just so that I could get my Dive Master's certificate, which would get me onto sea dives for free.

Yet, even though I was now totally put off deep diving and thought diving in caves was the height of idiocy, I had fallen in love with being underwater. I just couldn't get enough. Diving was a haven that allowed me to escape from, well, me. My personal life was this world of confusion, stress and fear in which I struggled on a daily basis to cope, never mind find any form of control. Diving was a place of peace and calm in which I excelled. I *needed* to be underwater just to remain sane.

Who I was when I started diving is as important as who I have become thanks to diving. There was a void in my life that created my need to dive. It was that need that propelled me ever deeper and deeper, regardless of my fear. It was a need that even today I do not fully comprehend. Perhaps it would be easy to blame everything on my childhood and parents. But that would mean I would have to answer the question of whether I had a difficult childhood, and I never have been able to say yes to that. How could I call my childhood and family difficult when there are people out there who have been in violent, abusive homes? By comparison my world was a walk in the park. All I was coping with was the aftermath of divorce and it just seemed embarrassing to never have been able to take that in my stride and move on.

I have been trying to understand who I am and why I made the choices I made for a long time now and somehow I always find myself back in my childhood, wondering who I would have been if I had different parents. I have always had the uncomfortable thought that my parents were never really the parents I seemed to need. How easy it would be just to blame who I was on the pair of them? Then nothing that followed would have been my fault.

I never managed to find peace with my dad, who was always able to bully me, even as an adult. His battle with alcohol didn't help matters, nor did his ability to turn everything into a drama that focused only on him. I loved my dad, but I didn't like him. My one constant memory is of being invisible in his world, as if I was never a daughter that he needed or at least, not the daughter that he got. After four unsuccessful attempts at suicide (the most notable ones being the one on my birthday and the one on New Year's Eve with my vacumn cleaner hose), his heart gave out and he died from a series of devastating heart attacks in 1998. That is the short story.

Talking about my mom is more difficult. I was the daughter she knew she would have when she was ten years old and my link to her was always strong. She was my lifeline yet ours wasn't a simple relationship. I loved her deeply but that made it hard to be angry with her or disagree with her. I battled to accept her breast cancer, never mind her long time boyfriend. She did however love me - very much. Especially after the divorce she always seemed so lost, needing help and support just to survive the life she found herself in. I was twelve when my parents got divorced and not only did I lose my father in a popularity contest (I sided with my mom, much to my dad's distress), I also lost my school friends to a new school, my house and devastatingly, the rest of my family who decided that divorce and Catholicism could not be reconciled and so everyone was ex-communicated.

Everything seemed to break when my parents got divorced. My brother (364 days younger than me) sided with my dad and we went from inseparable to bitter enemies. The combination of my parents and the drama of their divorce created this nagging thought that something was missing. Home never felt like family. It never felt safe. Diving felt like family was supposed to be – it felt safe.

Personally I was a mess and diving was what kept me going. I was paralysed by fear, emotionally disconnected and severely lacking confidence. Hard words to put on paper and hardly the description you would expect of someone who ends up with a world record. There are definitely days when I wish I could pretend I wasn't that person! Then again, perhaps if I had been different I would never have wanted to dive deep. I hate talking about who I was in my 20s (that is such a 30s thing to say – oh well…), but even though I was a mess in the 'real' world, when I was underwater all that fell away from me. I was just me and I was OK as me. Underwater was a haven - a quiet place where I had control. What was more, I was good at diving and it felt even better to finally find something that I enjoyed and could lose myself in.

My passion for diving consumed me, filling a void to which I was mostly oblivious. I made the decision to become an instructor simply because I felt that I would be a better diver if I had to know diving well enough to teach it. As I gained more confidence in my ability to dive, I started to look to where I could dive next and there was only one place left - down. I found myself once again wanting to see what is was like to be at the Police Sign. Depth no longer intimidated me, and the darkness?, Well, it had started to beckon.

Trying to get deeper was where I hit my first stumbling block. I couldn't. Not because I didn't have the ability or certification or training – that I had. I couldn't get permission.

I remember one dive in particular (a grid to grid that was the first on the long list of conditions you had to have met in order to do a

Police Sign). I had patiently fulfilled the requirements to get to that dive; in fact, I had more dives than Nuno required, so I really expected to be included when Nuno selected divers. When I wasn't, I was in shock! I simply couldn't understand what had just happened. Especially as I knew that one of the guys who had been allowed on the dive didn't have either the certificate or the number of dives I had been told were required. There was nothing concrete preventing me from going deeper and exploring (it would have been far easier if there was. If I had failed a certificate, or bent at 50 meters, then I would have a reason I could understand).

My skill and experience seemed to have nothing to do with it (everyone including Nuno had told me that I was an excellent diver, better than a lot of the guys); I wasn't on the dive simply because I was female. I was stunned and hurt. I doubt if Nuno even remembers the incident, yet that one dive seems to have created the tone of pretty much every dive for quite a long time thereafter. It took a great deal of drama and some serious convincing (which included blatant comparison to every one of the guys allowed to go) before it was clear that excluding me from that dive had no factual basis.

If any dive was definitive, that was. Here was something that I knew I was good at, and that the people in power wanted to deny me access to … and that made it impossible for me to refuse the challenge. I made a point of getting the experience I needed to compete with the men around me. My goal wasn't the world record (I didn't have that much confidence in myself), it was now Nuno's team.

It made sense. If I was trying to prove that I was as good a diver as anyone else (and I was), then the best way to do that was to get on Nuno's team. After all, he was the deepest man in Africa and the second deepest man in the world, so his dive team had to be the best, especially as it was practically impossible to get onto the team. If anything was exclusive Nuno's support team was. Which was really where my quest for depth started, trying to break in.

Breaking In

What started out as a passion for the sea had evolved into something more personal. Diving had become a challenge, or rather fitting into diving had become a challenge. Without really being aware of it I had I bet my entire concept of myself on one event happening – becoming one of Nuno's support divers. My desire to get on his team was about more than personal recognition though. Nuno and Sheck were doing what the world deemed impossibly risky and what is more, they were succeeding. Nuno seemed to be able to ignore public opinion and the established rules of how things were done; reconstructing what was known it into something brand new. Here was a real life hero, just like in my books. Even if I had not enjoyed diving I would have wanted to be part of his team just in the hope that some of his heroicness rubbed off on me. Heroes have courage, confidence and power. They know what they are doing. Heroes live their own lives on their own terms somehow escaping the battering that the rest of us have to endure.

Whilst I envied the strengths I attached to being a hero and explorer, I didn't see myself as one. The closest I could see myself getting was as a support diver. Heroes tend to be in the public eye and the thought of being so visible petrified me. I didn't want to have to justify myself. I certainly did not want to have to withstand the level of criticism and judgement that came along with the label. I just wanted to be part of something - I wanted to belong and contribute.

It is one thing knowing what it is you want, and entirely another working out how to get there. This was Nuno's world. He owned it, so if I was to break into it I needed to fit into it. Which was a problem because Nuno didn't invite women on his trips. Ever! There was a strict 'no girlfriend or wives' policy on these trips. The explanation was simple: he thought the wives and girlfriends got too emotional, contaminating the atmosphere, distracting the divers and creating a life-threatening risk. Ergo, no women on a deep diving expedition. The only exception was Nuno's wife Liz, who had learnt how to fit in.

I must have chosen the right approach because finally, after months of patient waiting and never stepping out of line on WUC trips, I was invited on Nuno's next dive. Even my supporters within Nuno's team were surprised. I had my opportunity and I wasn't going to blow it. Getting an invite was just the first hurdle. There was a list of people who had received a first invite but never a second one and I didn't want to be on that list - not after all the work I had put in.

Helping Records Get Broken

It was 1994 and Nuno's first dive to 230 meters at Boesmansgat. This was my first time at Boesmansgat and even after hearing so much about it, it was a surprise.

Boesmansgat is the third largest water filled cave in the world – a fact that is completely at odds with its location, smack bang in the middle of the flat semi-desert of the Northern Cape. One moment you are driving through scrub, avoiding wildebeest and springbok, the next you are at a small and totally unmemorable hillock where you stop. Everyone bails out of the vehicles and disappears into the brush. You look around and see … well brush. No immense and impressive body of water or anything. It is only as you follow the fast disappearing team that you realise what looked to be flat ground is in fact a huge sinkhole. Brush gives way to rock, which ends with a steep, high cliff. 100 meters below you is the hole itself and what looks like a very, *very* tiny piece of water.

The realisation hits that all (and I mean *all*) your diving kit has to be carried from way up here to way down there. To make it worse, as a support diver you are also required to get all the additional gear that Nuno will need for his dive to the water; that's only 15 extra cylinders at 20 kilograms a shot. And then, once you have carried everything down to the water's edge, you have to carry most of it back out again *every day* to be filled for the next day's diving.

I have never worked so hard in my life. Just walking to the water is a 20 minute endeavor that involves some serious rock scrambling. Walking out takes at least 30 minutes, most of it uphill. There was a high attrition rate on Nuno's trips and no clear-cut guidelines as to what to do to keep you in his good graces, but there was one thing I knew I couldn't afford to be - the weakest link. I had to pull my weight physically. I also couldn't afford to slip into the role of the emotionally 'weakest' link. No matter how tired I got, no matter how frustrated at being restricted to 20 meters even when I had the certification to dive deeper, I couldn't let anyone else know. This was all about one thing and one thing only … getting Nuno to his depth and back. I was getting good at suppressing who I was and being who the people around me needed me to be.

No matter whom you go with, your first trip to Boesmansgat is an initiation, both on a personal level and from the team's viewpoint. As support divers we would not actually be doing any major diving (that was Nuno's job), however that did not exempt us from experiencing both the physical and emotional side effects that come with being at Boesmansgat on a trip where one of us could die trying to get deeper. You're stuck on a hillside with no distraction but the task at hand. The team has to work together, because there is no other way to get a diver deep without people to fetch and carry (both in and out of the water). More importantly, the team must not be a distraction for the deep diver. He has to trust the people around him to do their jobs so that he can focus on his dive. His life depends on that focus.

My first trip to Boesmansgat was to be pivotal not only for my own diving, but also for Nuno's. This was the first time he would dive deeper than 200 meters and the first time he would spend almost 12 hours in the water. Up until then Nuno had gained a reputation for walking out of deep dives as if he had just gotten out of a bath. He seemed to suffer none of the normal tiredness that other divers routinely exhibited. I had spent a year watching and hearing about Nuno and how well he managed dives that other people suffered on, so I was not expecting this dive to be any different. We were all expecting him to simply walk out of the dive as if it was 20 meters, not sub-200.

This was my first time as a support diver and whilst I was finding support diving to be particularly uninspiring I could not help but fall in love with Boesmansgat. Up until then the whole deep diving thing hadn't really been real, but when I slipped through the cave entrance into the funnel that led to the cave proper, all I wanted to do was explore further. Instead, I was restricted to 30 meters and had to stay within an arm's length of a shot line that tantalisingly disappeared under the cave ceiling into the black heart of the main cave. I wanted to be going where the guys were going - over the edge at 60 meters and then down into the main hole to 100 meters. All of a sudden my boundaries and personal limits had expanded. I was no longer content being the shallow air support. I wanted to see and experience the dives that the guys were talking about. The seeds of discontent had been sown.

Not that I had much time to dwell on my own aspirations. With only 5 days to set up Nuno's deep dive we were busy almost continuously. If I was not lugging kit in and out, I was sitting next to a noisy compressor filling what seemed to be an endless supply of cylinders well into the night. And after all the furore of getting set up it was suddenly dive day and without a glance backwards, Nuno simply disappeared under the water and all we had left to do was wait.

After all the frenzy and activity to get to this point I found the sudden lack of activity disturbing. The reality of being a support diver was no longer something I could avoid - there was nothing to do but think and wonder as we waited. Had Nuno made it? Was he safely on his way back? I was learning what it means to be a support diver – you are the last person to know if the deep diver was successful. You have to wait, and wait, and then wait some more and all the time your mind is wondering "was that the last time I am going to see Nuno?"

The deep support diver would be the first person to find out if Nuno was on his way and if he had made his depth. The rest of us we would have to wait until he came out to find out the news. All in all it made for a long and tense two hours. We were all very relieved when we found out that Nuno was on his way up and that he had made 230 meters.

With that news we settled in for a long and cold day. As shallow support I was alternating 60 minute dives over five hours and it wasn't much fun. Firstly the water was cold and I was in a wetsuit, which means the longer the dive, the colder I got. There is also nothing to do or see other than Nuno, and he sleeps when he decompresses (there is nothing quite as boring as watching someone sleeping underwater). You sit and you watch and get colder and colder as the minutes wear by. It was a relief when Nuno got to his 6 meter stop. That at least meant we were out of the cave and had frogs to look at. Actually, the pond that provides access to the cave is quite spectacular underwater being covered in a wavy green carpet that is speckled with frogs in various stages of growth. With hours to spend waiting for Nuno to finish his decompressing and nothing much to do but practice breathing and buoyancy the day tends to be long and we were all very pleased when his dive finally ended and he surfaced. Mostly we were looking forward to the day being over and the chance to get a hot meal.

It wasn't to be! Nuno came out white and unable to move. He was quite literally exhausted and borderline hypothermic. We suddenly found ourselves in a situation we hadn't really planned for. As night settled in, we wrapped him in a silver emergency blanket in an effort to warm him up and waited. No one wanted to go back to camp and leave Nuno behind, so we tried to make ourselves comfortable on the surrounding rocks. Not that we had a lot of options. If he could not walk out himself we would have to put him onto the spine board and then manhandle him up the rocks to our camp, halfway out. Now, Nuno is not a small man. He does three hours of gym a day and is a national underwater hockey player. Think Vin Diesel with a Portugese accent and you have a pretty accurate description of Nuno. No one wanted to have to carry him out (to be honest, I am not sure we could have), so we waited and hoped that he would recover enough energy to walk out himself. It was well into the early hours of the morning when he finally managed the arduous climb back to the camp. We fell into bed to exhausted and too cold to even think of food.

We woke up the next day tired and not really looking forward to packing everything up. As we slowly emerged from our tents we heard the news that Nuno had developed a bend in his arm during the night - which meant one of us would be leaving early and driving him straight to the chamber to get treated. The good news was that his dive to 230 meters was a new African record. Even better, he was now only 20 meters behind Sheck. The official world record was well in sight and there was no stopping our exuberance.

Nuno's physical state coming out of the water had not evolved into anything serious and seemed to be more a result of hours decompressing without drinking or eating than anything else. It sounds obvious now that if you are spending a whole day underwater and subjecting your body to the extremes of deep diving you need to drink and eat to keep your energy levels up, but in those days only two people in the world had ever tried to do a dive that deep or for that long and a rehydration (let alone eating) schedule was simply not part of deep dive plans.

With 230 meters successfully under his belt there was no stopping Nuno and six months later he was planning another trip. He was always reluctant to tell anyone exactly what his planned depth was, but the rumour was he was aiming for 250 meters. I was praying that I had made the grade on the last trip and would be invited back again. Much to my relief I was.

The last trip had awakened in me a strong desire for deep exploration so when I heard that my depth limit had been lifted to 50 meters I was ecstatic. To get deeper I was planning on following the same route the other guys in the team had taken - Nuno's trips. Every year the support team would come back having gotten not only Nuno that much deeper but themselves too. My focus on this trip was a promised 75 meters. It would have to wait until Nuno had done his dive and it depended on him not using up all the helium, but I could barely contain my excitement.

A dive to 250 meters in 1994 was at the cutting edge of technical diving. Only Sheck Exley had been as deep so there was not much practical evidence to work with when creating a dive plan. Nuno had revised his dive plan based on his experiences from his last dive (and extensive discussions with Sheck and co), adding a hydration strategy and a re-heating plan to try and offset the sheer physical drain of a 12 hour dive. We were all confident that he would ace 250 meters. We were almost right - Nuno walked out of the dive smiling with lots of energy, albeit stone cold deaf having suffered an inner ear bend at 40 meters. It was rather an odd scene; there was nothing wrong with Nuno other then the fact that he couldn't hear anything, and unaccustomed to being deaf, every time he spoke to anyone he would assume we couldn't hear as well and so shout at us. We said goodbye to him as he was once again driven off to the chamber and re-focused – now we could dive for us.

You would laugh if you saw our kit back then. My twin cylinders (twins) were held together with ratchet straps (not the factory made metal bands I have these days). There were no technical bcs which meant I was using a standard sport bc (in my case a horse collar - they don't exist anymore so don't worry if you have no idea what it is). Many of the basics that we can't dive without today (like canister lights) were also non-existent (I was using a number of hand held torches that I mounted on a helmet as my light source).

We *were* diving using the concept of redundancy (always have a second source of life critical equipment), however non-existent equipment meant that we did not have the luxury of items like manifolds which allow you to access air from either of your cylinders when something goes wrong with one. Instead, we were doing it the old fashioned way (it was the normal way back then) - using independent twin sets and regularly changing dvs throughout the dive to ensure there was sufficient air in either cylinder to get us out if something went wrong. Without the edge that modern day equipment provides, surviving deep dives back then was totally dependant on skill and your ability to think underwater.

With the go ahead for a 75 meter dive and enough time and helium to get me there I was quietly optimistic - my excitement tempered by the nagging thought that getting to 75 meters might be as disappointing as my first 40 meter dive. What if I hated it? Worse, what if I bent? Bending in WUC's eyes was unforgivable and meant you did not know what you were doing. A bend would mean the end of my deep diving career for certain.

With mix in one cylinder, air in the other and two escorts I finally disappeared under the ceiling of the cave into the black void that is Boesmansgat. It was incredible; floating down a shot line into pure darkness, the light of the cave entrance gradually receding until it resembled two glittering jewels suspended in crystal clear water. Then even that disappeared as I slipped under the ceiling leaving only pure darkness and the sound of bubbles.

I walked away from that trip not only with a new personal depth record but a firm desire to get deeper. I loved being part of these trips - I loved the diving and I loved the fact that I was the only woman on the team. My struggle to get deep and be accepted seemed to be finally over. Now all that was left was diving.

But I want to be Deepest Too

I spent two years as part of Nuno's team and during that time the women's world record was always something that was around. I remember Nuno teasing me about it, saying "Come on Verna, there are no other women doing what you are doing" and initially it didn't seem to be a hard thing to do, sitting as it was at 120 meters (Mary Ellen Eckhoff). Then, Dr Anne Kristovich moved that depth to 167 meters which did not seem quite so easy a target. These numbers have lost their context in a world where more and more divers are breaking 200 meters, but in the early 90s I could count on one hand the number of divers who had been to 100 meters, never mind deeper. I had no doubt I could reach 120 meters, however 167 meters was a little more intimidating.

My involvement with Nuno's dives meant I was under no illusions that deep diving was easy. Reality is hard to avoid when you have to watch a man with as much physical strength as Nuno laid flat by a dive. Yet having access to one of the best divers in the world (not to mention support and equipment) put me in a unique position. With neither Eckhoff nor Kristovich actively diving sub-100 meters, there were no contenders for the women's title. The odds seemed stacked on my side and I finally acknowledged that I wanted to try for the women's world record.

Nuno was planning what was to be his final world record dive and I was looking forward to the opportunity to not only be there, but hopefully break 100 meters. I was training hard and diving at every opportunity but something was not quite right. On trips I was finding it harder and harder to get onto the teams that were going deep. When I didn't get an invite to Nuno's 280 meter expedition I was stunned. To make it worse not only was I not on his world record team, but I was also persona non grata within WUC. Finding dive buddies was suddenly very, very hard.

To this day I do not know what happened. All I can attribute it to was the fact that I had started to talk about wanting to be the deepest. Almost overnight Nuno went from teasing me about going after the record to intimating I was being over-confident. I was confused, frustrated and angry. More importantly I no longer had access to the support and knowledge that had made the women's world record appear within reach.

My one trimix dive (done under supervision) meant nothing. If I wanted to be deepest I was going to have to get below 75 meters on mix which meant I would have to get that elusive trimix certificate. It had taken me five years to get this far. Little did I realise that my next step, one more certificate, would take me almost as long again.

Being excluded by Nuno was one thing (and not actually unusual), but it came hand in hand with exclusion from my friends. Diving had gone from a place that felt like home to a place where I felt like an unwelcome stranger. Life had once again become a confusing muddle.

If it was the intention of my 'friends' to get me to change my mind about chasing the world record, they failed. I might not have known how I was going to get all the way there, but I knew what my first step was - my trimix certificate. Unfortunately the only person running trimix courses was Nuno.

It has always been hard for me to interact in circumstances in which I am uncertain of my place. Which meant that even though I managed to get myself onto the next trimix course, I could not get myself to actually attend anything more than the first lecture. It was only with the arrival in the club of Gilbert Gunn that I got momentum back. Gilbert was also finding it hard to break into the technical group but he did not suffer the same 'shyness' that was isolating me. Instead, he managed to convince Nuno to run another a trimix course and I made sure I was on it.

This time round I was determined not to be intimidated. I was also determined that by the time I had finished the course, I would know how to dive trimix. This isn't as easy as it sounds. Whilst I was on the course to learn, the rest of the guys already understood the course content and were there to get the official certificate. The lectures were a formality. You were not supposed to ask questions or expect detailed explanations, which would not have been a problem except for the fact that trimix is based on maths and physics (two subjects that I have always had to work very hard at) which meant that I was slow to understand. Even simple things like how to select a gas for a dive or work out how much helium and oxygen should be in a mix, were almost impossible for me to answer. Their impatience at my slowness did not help me learn any faster, nor did their approach - which was to simply take over and do it for me when I got stuck.

I remember one particular instance when I was working on my laptop trying to get my dive plan sorted. Instructors and fellow divers were firing instructions at me, to the point where one of them picked up my laptop and started to do the dive plan for me. I grabbed it back and practically shouted at him that I would never learn if I did not do it for myself and could he just help me rather than do it for me. The response from the audience was amusement which would ordinarily have embarrassed me so much I would have given in and just let them do it for me, but not this time. This time I would not be the damsel in distress.

My stubbornness paid off and on New Year's Day 1999 I finally made 100 meters. I was elated and with my last obstacle gone Gilbert and I immediately started to plan to dive deeper - without Nuno's sanction but not without his influence. With few

books and no courses to teach us we were doing it Nuno's way –
we were learning as we dived.

By then Gilbert had caught the deep diving bug and had
the number 220 meters in his head. My number was 185 meters
and we planned our first step, a dive to 120 meters. We had hoped
to find that depth in the world's largest natural sinkhole, Guinas
Lake in Namibia. Guinas Lake is yet another of those oddities, one
of the largest inland lakes smack bang in the middle of the
Namibian desert. Even though we were there in winter it was
stinking hot, climbing to 40 °C during the day. Shade was sparse
and the water a 100 meter sheer vertical drop away and not a stair
in sight. We had to navigate a rope ladder into the water and haul
all our kit up and down using pulleys. Once our kit was at water
level we had to retrieve it and get into it whilst floating, not an easy
task when you are wearing a dry suit and you have your bc inflated
to prevent your cylinders from sinking.

I have memories of heat, sun, grey dust, cold beer and sore
muscles from that trip, and spectacular diving. From the white
sandy bottom at 100 meters, you could look up and see the divers
getting kitted on the surface. Decompressing was made a whole lot
more interesting by the shoals of colourful fish that swarmed over
the walls. We were not there to sightsee though; we were looking
for depth with each of the four dive teams taking a new section of
the lake and running the depth finder over it. After almost a week
of diving Gilbert and I picked out a spot that we thought would

give us our target of 120 meters. It would require some swimming but we were not fazed. We were however, to be disappointed. Even though we stretched the dive by 2 minutes we never did find the back of the cavern we were exploring.

Smooth white sand simply reached out in front of us with no end in sight and only shoals of small white fish to break the monotony. After minutes of swimming we had reached 117 meters and it looked like we would need at least another 5 minutes to get the three meters we were missing. We were out of time and already eating away at our reserve gas so we had no choice but to turn around.

That dive stuck with both of us. Instead of the traditional and 'boring' deep bounce we had been aiming at, we were now hooked on exploration. We wanted to search for depth in new places and that meant one place, the last level of Badgat.

Our goal was still 120 meters and the only place outside of Boesmansgat where we thought we might get it was a rumoured incline shaft at Badgat. Our choice was as much driven by the desire to explore as it was by convenience. Whilst Boesmansgat would have guaranteed us the depth, we would have to take all our own equipment (including compressors). Badgat however, had an established technical shop that supplied gas and extra equipment.

These days Badgat is synonymous with technical diving in South Africa and is really our only easily accessible site. It is a flooded asbestos mine with a number of levels and interconnected passageways that make it the perfect technical dive site, presenting divers with plenty to explore as these interconnected levels and tunnels make it more of a challenge to explore than Boesmansgat, especially if you want to dive deep.

Every dive at Badgat starts in the open water of the now flooded quarry. From there your reference point is a confused mass of tree roots that cascade from the cliff five meters above you. The entrance to the tunnels is marked by a mass of boulders at 16 meters. This gives you access to the first level which connects directly to the main shaft - a 100 meter swim away. The main shaft descends vertically another 100 meters past a number of other levels that extend outward: second level at about 25 meters, third level closer to 35 meters, seventh level at 80 meters.

The drop down the main shaft is visually interesting and not without its obstacles, with steel bars dissecting the space and the old steel ladders criss-crossing the one sidewall. There is still a lot of iron in the water, creating elegant rust stalagmites that crumble into silt under the inevitable bubble stream. Getting to the bottom of the main shaft is a bit disappointing - there is nothing to see but a silt pile and there is only one way to go, the last level. Because of its depth, this last level took over five years to be explored. What they found was disappointing, a single blind tunnel with no large side tunnels as was the case with the other levels. They did report seeing a hole in the wall some 3 minute's swim into the tunnel. They thought it might descend further and they were right. Named the incline shaft (even though it is more accurately a decline) this is the only location in South Africa other than Boesmansgat that can get you to 185 meters.

Because of its depth and swim, no one had wanted to explore the incline but Gilbert and I could see no good reason why not to. The problem was the swimming at 110 meters, more specifically, the swim back for 3 minutes after reaching our planned 120 meters. In all we would be sub-100 meters for over 10 minutes which was totally contrary to the established 'get deep and get out as fast as possible' strategy that most deep divers were employing. We would also be exerting ourselves at depth, which made the risk of decompression seem almost a certainty.

Yet the appeal of being the first person to see where this incline went was too tempting and in 2000 we found ourselves at 121 meters in a small tunnel heavily laden with silt. The predictions that the tunnel would simply end turned out to be untrue and at 121 meters it looked like we had barely penetrated the incline shaft. I was excited when we got back to the surface, already planning our next dive to 145 meters and wondering if the incline would get us there but it was not to be and shortly afterwards Gilbert made the decision to stop deep diving.

I was back at square one.

(3) Courage is Hard to Come By

What was keeping me going when the world seemed set on keeping me from what I wanted? Was it the challenge that drove me? Or was it something deeper? Something missing inside me that I just could not acknowledge? I know this much: there was no single moment that got me to this point. One moment I was diving for joy and the next it was a challenge I could just not walk away from. The world had decided I was not good enough to be the deepest and I had to prove them wrong.

The millennium had started out well (I had reached my next step of 121 meters) and then it just fizzled out. In no way had my desire to get deep enough to beat the women's world record disappeared. If anything, it had just become stronger. The more the world beat me down, the more stubborn I became. I would be deepest, if it was the last thing I did. All I had to do was find a way to get there - a way from here to there. How hard could it be?

But my ambition did not match my level of experience and knowledge which left me in a decidedly odd place. Was it presumptuous to think that I could break the world record and compete with the men? My so-called friends seemed to think so, but what was it I was supposed to do? How was I supposed to behave? Was I supposed to pretend that I didn't want to try for the world record so that I would be accepted and then follow the traditional route of waiting to be given permission to dive deeper? Was it really that simple?

My problem with that approach was it allowed Nuno and his team of 'expert' support divers to define what I was capable of - a process that is soul destroying especially when you are surrounded by people who do not see you and never acknowledge you, never mind a team where chances to prove yourself are hard won. To make matters worse I was leaving a six year relationship that had in itself been dramatic and soul destroying. Not only was I now outside of Nuno's team, I was also single and my friends were turning out to be thin on the ground.

Fighting for every meter was energy intensive and with Gilbert leaving I would either have to find a new buddy or find a new way to move forward. It sounded a whole lot easier to just wait until the next batch of divers were trained and then pick one or two who were interested in deep diving and work on getting them training and experience, but did I really want to be reliant on another buddy? It seemed like all I was doing was training divers that sooner or later were poached by another deep team, leaving me right back at the beginning.

The upside of being forced to make the decision to remain independent was that I no longer had to jump through hoops chasing an ever changing set of rules (admittedly, they gave me something to do even though they got me nowhere). Yet I hardly seemed to be any better off. It would have been far simpler if I had just been content with waiting in the shadows for permission to get deeper. Not that I am sure that permission would ever have arrived, but I would still have had my 'friends' and the life I knew.

Instead I was in a self-imposed limbo: there was no way I was going to swallow my pride and beg help from the man himself. In my dreams I was abandoned on a black, barren rock surrounded by a violent sea. I knew where I needed to get to, I just could not find my first step.

Oblivious to my dilemma a different drama was unfolding. Whilst doing a 100 meter dive at Sodwana (one of the more popular South African coastal dive sites) a deep diver had died. His name was Denis Harding.

Denis had been on what should have been a simple ocean dive and his death came as an unwelcome shock (as death always does). He had been an experienced diver and a gentle man leaving behind a young family which somehow made the situation even more tragic. I had not been a close friend of Denis's (we were occasional diving buddies and I had enjoyed the dives that I had done with him), yet his death touched me. It seemed fitting to attend his funeral but I didn't feel that I knew Denis well enough to gatecrash his funeral. Not that I expected his funeral to be a quiet family affair. When a diver dies (especially one who was as well known as Denis) the whole diving community turns up and I found myself parking at the church, never really having made the decision to attend. I felt uncomfortable going. Firstly it was a funeral, then on top of that I would have to face former friends and play nice for the cameras; a level of socially accepted insincerity that does not sit well with me. Yet for some reason I could not explain, being there was important.

Listening to the pastor talk about Denis and his passion for life made me start to question how I was living my own life. What would the pastor say at my funeral? That I lived a long and unhappy life, never really doing what I wanted because I was so afraid of being judged?

As the pastor tried to give solace and find meaning in Denis' death, he said something that I just could not ignore. Denis had died doing what he loved. The words stuck and with a sudden clarity I knew that I was here for a reason. As I listened to the pastor talk I heard the story of a life that was lived so completely differently to the way I was living mine. Denis had loved life and had made the most of the days he had been given, whereas I was still waiting - wasting my life.

I have long thought that some deaths are more powerful than others - as if the quality of a person's life is measured in some way by the number of people they touch both while they were alive and then in that final moment of death. I walked into the church in a state of turmoil. I walked out with an eerie sense of calm and peace. I could not let Denis' death be something that just faded away. It had to have some meaning, some impact.

I had been searching for my next step yet I had always known the answer, I just had never liked it. Thanks to Denis it no longer seemed right to stay stuck in my own misery just because I was scared. I had to stop feeling sorry for myself and get on with it. I was going to have to do this on my own, without a Nuno to take responsibility. I knew then that if I died tomorrow I would regret never having tried to go deeper. As I made my way back to the office I silently made a commitment to do whatever it took - no matter how uncomfortable or scary. I would no longer drive myself insane by doing the same thing over and over again and expecting a different result.

It turned out to be ridiculously simple. New Years was just around the corner and for the first in what was a long time I reviewed the year that had disappeared, trying to find out what I had done with those 365 days. Not a whole lot as it turned out. I knew I had been busy but as usual had nothing to show for it.

What I needed was something concrete to aim for, so I made three New Year's resolutions; one easy (just to get some practice), one kind of difficult and then the real hard one. I had to have accomplished at least one of these resolutions this time next year! Just one! I figured even I could manage that!

So I took up belly dancing with my newly arrived niece and discovered the joy of looking like a complete idiot in front of a bunch of strangers. I started to write, a passion I had locked away, terrified that the words would come out wrong. And I started to create my next dive plan. This time there would be no excuses, no migraines, no flu. This year I was determined that there would be only me to blame. It didn't matter how much closer I got (I wasn't even realistically expecting to get diving), it just mattered that I went ahead in spite of my fear.

New Ways to Do Old Things

It was a great relief to have something concrete to aim at. By not stressing about what I did not have I was now able to focus on how to make what I did have work, which in turn meant it was a whole lot easier to focus on the all important dive plan.

The dive plan is the framework on which the dive hangs and as such, defines the basic parameters of a dive, namely how long I will be underwater (bottom time) and how deep I will go. From these I can calculate out how much gas I will need to get to my depth and (more importantly) back, always ensuring I have enough gas in reserve to manage a catastrophic gas loss. This calculation gives me my critical gas pressure and is the third parameter of a dive plan. Practically speaking, the critical pressure is a turning point on the dive – when I reach it I have to turn around. If I continue descending I start to breathe gas that is allocated to getting me back up, which means I face the very real possibility of running out of gas, especially if something goes wrong.

A good dive plan gives you an edge because it allows you to dive without having to think about the basics. If something goes wrong you have free mental capacity that allows you to focus on what is happening at that moment. Yes, you can succeed with a bad dive plan, but your chances are not good as you are relying totally on your abilities and plenty of luck.

There was one thing I had to do before I started on my dive plan though. I needed to get Joseph Emmanuel on board. Joe had always been a good friend. We had met on Nuno's support dives and somehow stuck. He is not the expected hard-core, macho man that one expects from a technical diver. I can never think of Joe without getting an image of Mr Bean in my head (although I have to quickly add that the resemblance is purely physical). When I told him that I was determined to go deeper and was planning a dive that year, and asked him if he would act as support, he did not hesitate. I was immensely relieved and planning to rely on the strength of his personality to offset my own weaknesses - the biggest of which was going to be a relentless 'can do' attitude.

Instinctively I knew that to be successful I would need someone with more distance and perspective involved in creating the final dive plan. I needed someone who I trusted and most importantly, someone to whom I would listen. I was betting that this second pair of unbiased eyes would give me an edge. My dive plan would have to be practical, which would mean I would have to be selective when it came to the risks that I would be managing, instead focusing on a set of more probable risks and discarding the rest. But which ones to discard and which to keep? A simple decision to not focus on line traps on my personal kit by say, taping my fin straps, could be lethal – I could find myself trapped at depth and at depth you do not have large amounts of time to solve problems – at depth your gas lasts mere minutes.

Together Joe and I created a nice balance. Joe's style was slower, tending toward thorough (hence his nickname SloMo) and definitely conservative. On top of which, he was good friends with Nuno. Having him on board meant I could indirectly get Nuno's advice. Which (to my surprise) Nuno gave freely. It made me wonder if my exile wasn't so much a personal thing, but a political necessity that gave Nuno 'plausible deniability'. If something went wrong and I died, his reputation wouldn't be tarnished.

My goal was 185 meters but my deepest dive was only 120 meters. Could I go straight to 185 meters or did I need a stepping stone? I was favouring a single dive of 145 meters followed by the world record attempt. My choice of 145 meters was based largely on the fact that I could get that depth from Badgat. Anything deeper and I would have to go to Boesmans and I did not have the resources for that. The recommendation that came back was 130 meters. Apparently, you should not increase your depth by more than 10 meters a year. Naturally I asked why. I had no intention of satisfying my critics by dying on this dive so I wanted to understand what the impact of a bigger jump would be. Would it kill me or could I jump faster? To my surprise there did not seem to be any concrete justification for a 10 meter depth increase. The only reason that emerged was that it was safer.

These days I understand the principle better. When you push your own limits you are looking for the edge that separates staying alive from dying. It is easy to shoot past that line. Which is not a problem if you have not wandered too far past. However, when you take too big a step the chances are good you may never find your way back.

You never know what you do not know so the trick is to find a jump that does not add too many new things all at once. This approach follows an old adage I remember from early on in my training - never add more than one new element to a dive. New means you are having to work at your dive and invariably that means your mind is occupied, trying to cope with something unfamiliar. You are now one step into the three strike rule. Now when the something goes wrong you can still cope, but you are also at your coping limit and should at this time turn the dive and get out of the water (always, always abandon the dive when the second thing goes wrong). The third strike rule takes into account how well your mind can cope with multi-tasking – with one new element on a dive you are busy, add a problem like a leaking power inflator and you are still coping, just. When the third thing goes wrong your mind is overloaded and you are no longer coping. Sooner or later you forget to manage one of the three problems you are sitting with and at that point the chances of getting out the water alive become seriously impaired.

In my case the new element I was adding was depth and no one could tell you how much deeper was in fact too deep. To complicate matters, the size of the increments that are deemed safe become smaller the deeper you go. Jumping from 50 meters to 100 meters is do-able (not recommended, but do-able). Jumping from 200 meters to 250 meters? Well, that has a tendency to kill people. As you go deeper the size of the jump has to decrease simply because as you go deeper the amount of time and mental capacity you have to deal with new elements is reduced. It becomes harder to manage situations at depth. However, the closer you get to your target depth the more impatient you are to get there and the more likely it is that you will bite off more than you can chew.

There is a balance between pushing to get to your goal and taking your time so that you can learn and get there safely.

Unfortunately, in order to find that balance you need patience, perspective and discipline. Patience had never been something I was good at and as for perspective, well, when you have spent all your life trying to get something it is easy to throw it all away in one last effort to succeed. Climbers call it summit fever and I was hoping that Joe was my cure.

Ten meter increments would ensure I would not overshoot my edge by too much but they still seemed way too conservative (at that rate it would take almost a decade to get where I wanted to be and I had no intention of taking that much time). I decided to stick to my original depth which was 20 meters deeper than my all time deepest dive. 20 meters was a number that didn't seem that daunting. It was also only 40 meters away from the record, so the record was one, maybe two dives away.

Which left the other major decision, the date of the dive. I picked an early date, Easter 2001 and only a couple of months away.

Was I ready?

I had been diving every other weekend for over a year trying to get deeper so there was no reason to delay until the second half of the year simply to get more in-water time. Besides, by diving earlier in the year I would have the second half of the year to try again. I also did not want to give myself enough time to rationalise this and come up with solid sounding excuses to put the dive off indefinitely. Mentally getting to the water was going to be tough, so the less time spent waiting, brooding and obsessing the better.

With the depth decided I could go ahead with the rest of the dive plan. I was planning to dive at Badgat and as soon as Nuno heard that, he started a concerted effort to get the dive moved (to Boesmansgat). I could not argue with the fact that the safest way to get deep was to bounce (go straight down and then come straight back up) and that I could only do that at Boesmansgat. However, it was a logistical no go. I would need compressors and cylinders and shot lines and experienced divers, none of which I had. That left Badgat and the incline shaft. From a logistical view point it was perfect being both accessible and with a dedicated dive shop on site however, from a technical difficulty and risk viewpoint it was the more dangerous of the two.

I felt that I had an advantage though - I was one of only three people to have dived the incline shaft so I had some idea of what I was getting into, even if Nuno did think it was mad. All that remained was to get as solid a dive plan as I could. I needed to get a list of risks and I reasoned the only way to do that would be by asking the question "why?"

"Why must I have continuous support from at least 100 meters?" I asked.

"Because," came the reply.

"Because of what?" I asked. "Is it because that is the way it has always been done and because it has proven successful so far?"

Silence was my answer. I was slowly realising that a lot of current diving practices existed for no other reason than that they worked. Not many people had questioned either why they worked or why they had come into being in the first place. The closest comparison I had from which I could learn was Nuno, however the differences between us were significant: I only had two support divers and my own personal kit with which to plan as opposed to a team of eight people and access to compressors and 15 odd extra cylinders and dvs. Physically I was also not Nuno Gomes which meant that even if I did everything else exactly as he did, my body might just not be up to the depth. I was counting on being able to reverse-engineer Nuno's principles and adjust them to my dive. Once I had those bare principles I could look at finding other solutions, solutions that fitted what I had. I left Nuno behind (which felt like taking a huge step of the edge of a large, high cliff) and trusted that I would either find something to stand on or learn how to fly.

Before I knew it, Easter was upon me. I packed up and drove to Badgat all the while petrified almost to the point of paralysis. The list of reasons why I shouldn't do this dive was long and impressive. It certainly wouldn't have come as a surprise to anyone back in Johannesburg if I decided to pack up and go home. In fact, they all thought that was the only sane decision to be made and maybe that would have been an option if I had not broadcast to the world my intention. I had to go through with this if I wanted to retain any self-respect, never mind respect from people who had been hearing over and over again how deep I wanted to go but not seeing anything.

The plan was to take a week getting the stage cylinders in place and doing the all-important practice dives, and it turned out to be a most miserable week indeed. I was obsessed with trying to find the thing that could kill me, worried that I had not planned for it so I would go over the dive again and again, trying to find what I had missed. Thank heavens for Joe's patience. Then there was the weather to contend with. Easter is normally hot and dry, except for this year. We found ourselves camping in torrential, almost continuous, rain. Every day I would look at the weather and say to myself "Maybe God is trying to tell me that it is not right? Maybe I should just pack up and go home?" It took enormous effort to stay put and remain focused on getting through that day. I was wondering if I was wasting my time and the only reason why I carried on with our plan was because I figured I could always decide not to do the actual dive on the day, but it would be really stupid if I got to the planned dive day and decided I wanted to dive and couldn't because none of the prep work had been done. Then I really would have only one choice - not dive.

Saturday came and with it another diver, Larry Holding. I now had three support divers. Then the rain lifted. It promised to be the first day all week with some sun. Things were looking up. The guys started to get kitted up and I still did not know if I was going to do the dive. I told myself I could not let the guys down so I would just get into the water, do the descent and then see how I felt. I could turn around then and not lose face. I got kitted up and joined them. To all intents and purposes, the dive was on.

There is no point in describing the swim along to the main shaft. It was long and took all of the 8 minutes I had allocated to it. The descent to the bottom of the main shaft was equally uneventful and once there, it seemed daft to turn around so soon. After all, I would still have to do the full decompression and would be wasting time and gas - both of which I had plenty of. I decided to just swim to the incline and turn around there.

I had hardly started the swim when I took a breath and almost nothing came out. I had planned to use one of my side slung cylinders for this portion of the dive, leaving my two back mounts for the last portion of the descent and so ensuring that I had plenty of air at the most dangerous point of the dive. Instead, the side sling had run out of air within a minute of the three minute swim. I could feel panic approaching as I grabbed my other dv and quickly changed to my still full back cylinders. With great relief my next breathe was normal. I had not stopped swimming but now started to wonder if I had missed the incline whilst I was changing dvs. The start of the shaft is not easy to find, being a rather insignificant collection of boulders that hide an almost invisible hole in the wall. I had time, but not enough to start swimming up and down looking for the entrance to the shaft. With panic not far away I could feel myself starting to breathe faster.

"Slow down, deep breath in, deep breath out," I told myself and swam on, eagerly looking for the entrance. Just as I was giving up hope it appeared in front of me. I swam over the boulders into the mouth and paused.

The view from the top of the shaft is intimidating. It's tiny, with just enough space for two divers to swim side by side. It is also covered in silt and hard to navigate thanks to the decline. If you knelt on the floor you could almost touch the ceiling which makes swimming difficult, especially if you don't want to kick up the silt. And you do not want to stir up silt. You need to be able to see what is ahead of you so you can avoid the mining junk scattered throughout the length of the shaft. The last thing I wanted was to get trapped on a piece; in the incline you are totally alone with your nearest support diver waiting at the bottom of the main shaft, high above you and a 3 minute swim away.

I convinced myself that an extra 10 meters would not be too much of a stretch and started my final descent. Somewhere in that next 10 meters my fear retreated and was replaced by calm. I remember getting to 120 meters and checking both my time and spg (gas contents gauge). I had plenty of time left to make 145 meters and I had plenty of gas so there was no 'proper' reason to turn back. Then came a sudden almost paralysing fear. Years of having it drilled into me that you only turn a dive because you have run out of time or gas or reached your depth kicked in - being petrified simply wasn't a good enough reason to turn around.

I switched my mind back off and focused on the job at hand, negotiating the beams and fallen metal that littered the shaft. Now was not the time to obsess about things going wrong. Joseph was waiting for me 10 minutes away and I didn't want to put him in the position of having to decide to extend his dive to try and find me or leave without me if I didn't make it back.

Before I knew it, I was at 145 meters. I tried to slow down slowly to avoid kicking up silt and then carefully turned around and got the hell out of there. Never was the sight of Joe at 100 meters more welcome. I was not celebrating yet though. I still had another five hours in the water and I could bend at any time, especially as I had been swimming at depth (something dive tables are not designed to cater for). Did I add enough extra safety in? Would I bubble? When? There were large portions of the dive during which I was alone. Joe had just done 100 meters for 10 minutes and so could not dive again. Peter had met me at 50 meters and then left at 30 meters having racked up deco and so also could not dive again. That left Larry who popped in every 30 minutes or so to see if I was still OK. If I bent while I was still in the cave I would have to manage until Larry got there. Not that there would be much he could do. I still would have to swim myself out into the open hole and still have to try and finish the rest of my decompression. Every tweak and every twinge of a muscle was carefully inspected – was this a bend? The hours passed and I got colder and colder, even in my dry suit. The only relief to the monotony was the annoying beeping of my Aladin dive computer. These were air only computers that told me my depth and calculated decompression based on me breathing air and not the trimix I had actually used. This meant that the decompression profile they generated was completely different to the trimix schedule I was actually on, requiring me to spend much more time in the water. As I moved up they started beeping at me, telling me to go back down and decompress. I had forgotten to switch computers to avoid exactly that problem and so had to wait until Larry came down to check on me to get him to take my bent computer away and give me a new one. Finally, I was into my last hour which is always the worst. You are 2 meters from the surface and stuck there until the deco is over. And then my five and a half hours was up. I surfaced and was barely able to contain my excitement.

I had done it! I had successfully dived deep on my own, with no permission. Now all I had to do was get through the next twelve hours without bending - then I could really relax. Everything went well until I woke up on Sunday very tired with very sore joints. Not willing to admit that I might be bent I ignored both, asking the guys to help me load up gear as I was simply too tired to. It is just one of those things - divers never admit to being bent. Having to go to a decompression chamber because your body decided to let you down is just not something that is easy to admit, especially when you have not broken any of the rules and especially not on this dive where getting it 100% right was so important. If I bent this shallow I would have a question over my head should I decide to go deeper. I sucked it up and told no one. I knew what it was like to bend for real, having had the misfortune of a shoulder bend sometime previously and this was nothing like that pain. If it got that bad I would go to the chamber, but not until then.

The dive had been hard. Far harder both mentally and physically than I had expected, but I couldn't suppress my elation. I had done something that every voice around me had told me I couldn't do. I had finally found the course to listen to myself and not the world and it had worked. The world record was in sight and I still had over half a year left. I was looking forward to reaching New Years having over achieved on my simple new years resolution of getting deeper, but what happened next stunned me – I found myself with an official sponsor, half of Nuno's support team and an equipment sponsor, Scubapro. I also found myself with a date for a record attempt, October. All I had been aiming for was to maybe get slightly deeper than 120 meters, not this!

Getting Started

There I was, suddenly surrounded by eager support divers and a company willing to throw hard cash at covering expenses. All

I had to do was get my head into the dive. Which was actually not that difficult - all I could think about was the dive. I was lucky if I got 3 hours sleep as a result. In the back of my head a voice kept on telling me that just because my last dive had been successful didn't mean the next one would be. In fact, there was even more on the line this time round - now I had an entire team of people who would be let down if I got this wrong.

An entire team. The phrase sang in my head. I had a team, finally! And not just any team. Some careful thought had gone into selecting the team members. Not only was I looking for people who could offset my weakness, I was also looking for people for who wanted to be on this dive as much as I did - people who would support my efforts to get deep.

Joseph Emmanuel and Peter Zachariou were a no-brainer. Just like last time, Joe would be my balance, and advisor and Peter would be watching over me in the water. This dive had to happen at Boesmansgat which is why I approached two of Nuno's team members, Craig Kahn and Craig Newham, both of whom I had always gotten on well with. In addition, I had four new divers who had no cave diving experience but plenty of enthusiasm; Derek Hughes (a long time friend and work colleague), John de Wet (my project manager and someone who had taken the time to support me both in diving and the workplace), Gareth Lowndes (the chairman of WUC) and Theo van Eeden (a police diver who was supplying hoses and lines).

Bringing divers onto a deep team who didn't have a cave or deep qualification *and* who had not dived at Boesmansgat before was controversial to say the least. But then, it wasn't like I had a huge pool of divers to work from. There are simply not a lot of cave divers out there and I made the decision to take people I knew and trusted and teach them what they needed, rather than take the risk of bringing along a trained diver whose attitude destroyed the team and jeopardised the dive. I wasn't looking for divers who would bring their own agendas and hijack the dive. Besides, I had just done five and half hours in the water with three divers, so the chances were good that I could manage around any training weaknesses in my support divers.

With the team selected we started the job of diving. Not only did we have to get three divers deep and cave qualified, I also had to hone my own diving skills until diving was something that didn't require my conscious attention. Practice, practice and more practice is the only way I have ever felt comfortable on dives like this. When I get in the water I need to believe that I know what I am doing. We figured we needed at least eight weekends to get everything and everyone up to speed, and with two months too cold to dive that set our dive date at October. We would be diving every other weekend until then.

With the deadline so close I found my perspective starting to shift. I might not be alive in three months and it mattered that I did not leave behind any regrets or unsaid words. Which was odd because for the longest time life had been something that wasn't so much fun and something I wouldn't miss. Not that I wanted to kill myself (that moment had passed almost as soon as it had come), but I wasn't going to actively fight to carry on living. I started to say my goodbyes and tie up loose ends. I started to do things that previously would have petrified me – after all I had nothing to lose; I might be dead in a couple of weeks.

Damsel in Distress? Not!

And then our time was up and the only thing left was the dive. I had spent every day until then going over every detail, trying to make sure that I had thought of pretty much everything. I had even made the trip two weeks long instead of one to give us enough time to manage any last minute problems.

A lot was riding on this expedition including my reputation as a diver and the reputations of the divers who had chosen to support me. It was important to get it right. It was as important not to die (no way was I prepared to give my critics that satisfaction). Needless to say, the universe has a sense of humour and had already started to test my resolve. First, Derek Hughes couldn't make it. His mother was critically ill and the entire family was waiting anxiously at her bedside. Then, the day after we arrived, I came down with the worst bout of food poisoning I have ever had. I was looking at a five and a half hour dive and for the first three days of the trip I could barely eat or get out of bed.

We had allocated just over a week to get everything set up, allowing two attempts at the dive in the following week (the Wednesday or the Friday) but nothing was going smoothly. None of our gas had arrived which left us with a dozen stage cylinders that needed to be filled and then placed in the water at specific depths *before* I did my dive. These stage cylinders were critical. Without them I wouldn't have enough gas to breathe for five hours. Filling takes hours and we had planned a full 4 days to get this all done, allowing me a day to get a deep dive in followed by a day off to recover and then *the* deep dive. With no oxygen or helium in sight we were suddenly looking at going home. Finally, we located the gas (100 kilometers away in Kimberleigh) and even though promises were made, by the Wednesday it still had not been delivered. I was simply not prepared to give up, even if it meant taking our private vehicles and spending a day driving backwards and forwards just to keep us on schedule. Luckily, before we had to resort to that, the gas arrived.

That was the least of my problems however - team dynamics were starting to become problematic. Instead of a friendly collaborative dictatorship (with me as the benevolent dictator), I seemed to have become the damsel in distress who should not bother her pretty little head over … well anything really. Being sick wasn't helping as it meant that I wasn't at the evening meetings where the day's issues were discussed and the next day's task list set. In my absence, two of the team had simply taken over the trip. Having a strong anathema to conflict I was starting to battle to get out of bed in the morning, never mind get up, smile and go and talk to people.

In their minds, nothing I was doing was right! I had to explain my entire dive plan to these self-appointed experts who would then decide if it was adequate or not and what changes they were going to make. Everything, *everything* I had been trying to avoid was suddenly right here. I appreciated the fact that if something went wrong and I died the entire team would be held accountable but I had not agreed to hand over responsibility for my life to anyone else.

Then to make everything worse, it was suddenly announced that the record had already been broken and was now sitting at 211 meters. I was now sitting on a fully sponsored dive to break a world record that had already been broken. It made sense for me to challenge my depth, trying to work out if it would be feasible to get to 215 meters this time round. Which was breaking my number one rule - don't change the dive plan and get tempted to dive deeper. But it was just so tempting: I was here, everything was set up and it was only an extra 20 meters I needed. To top it all off, this might be the chance I got to dive deep and I needed to walk away from the trip knowing that I had stuck to 185 meters because it was really the right thing to do and not just the safest thing to do. With the news that I was actively discussing the possibility of going deeper, things turned from bad to ugly! It was only Friday and either I was going to walk off or the Craigs were.

Which is when Derek arrived: there had been nothing they could do at his mother's bedside other than wait, so he had made the tough decision to pick up his life again and join the trip. Instead of a trip he could lose himself in, he found a trip that was about to come apart. Whilst the Craigs refused to listen to me, they did listen to Derek. He took over our evening meetings and played liaison, talking both sides off the precipice. The trip was now officially in an uneasy truce. My nose was firmly out of joint and I was actively refusing to be told what to do - it was my life on the line and they had no right.

All in all, not my proudest hour. I lost two good friends on that trip. Not that it mattered at that point. The only thing that mattered was doing the dive. I would not leave this trip without having tried everything to get to 185 meters. There could simply be no excuses for not succeeding. None!

And all the while, over and over and over in my head I was doing the dive - practicing, practicing, practicing. I needed to know it off by heart. I needed to be able to do this without thinking. I practiced the dive going well and then I practiced the dive going wrong. I practiced every scenario I could think of until no matter what happened, in my head, I could manage it.

Dive Day - Getting It Done!

Dogged persistence paid off and we finally we made our first scheduled record dive day with all team members still on board and everything ready to go. It was now up to me. We had to start the dive early (which I hate) so that there would be enough light at the end of the dive to get me evacuated in case I bent. We had planned for bends in water and out with a full time diving doctor (Dr Hermie Britz from DAN (Divers Alert Network)) on site plus a portable decompression chamber and a helicopter on standby.

Dive day dawned and no one knew quite how to deal with me, so they avoided me. Which was OK as I was equally out of my depth and avoiding them. Do you say goodbye? Do you say good luck? I just wanted it to be over. I certainly did not want anyone to make my nerves any worse than they already were. My head was already in the dive so Gareth drove me to the water, music blaring. This was it. I started to kit up with my heart racing. Not a good sign. When I'm diving I count on being calm, and being able to control my heart rate.

About the only thing I remember from that dive was how fast my heart was beating. As I started to descend the carefully laid shotline I realised that I had not taken enough weights with me. I was too light, which meant that I was taking too long to get down. I started to worry that I would run out of time, which would mean turning around without making my depth. Something I wasn't prepared to do. And all the time I was watching and waiting for something to go wrong. Even though I had practiced it, the thought of losing a cylinder on the way down scared me. Would I be able to keep on the line? The shotline was my lifeline. It connected me to the safety of the surface and all my support divers. If I lost the line I would be dead. If I stayed on the line would I have enough air left to get myself to my support divers who had extra gas? Would my dvs work that deep? They had been rated but never used that deep before. As I sunk into the blackness doubts and worries hovered at the edge of my consciousness. Slowly my focus turned to the dive and the shotline.

Before I knew it I was at 185 meters – and not stopping. Because I had been battling to sink I had not wanted to add air to my bc. I had been warned not to leave it too late because the deeper I went the longer it would take not to mention the more air I would need in order to stop. I had however done just that,

The Team
• Joseph Emmanuel
• Craig Kahn
• Craig Newham
• John de Wet
• Derek Hughes
• Theo van Heerden
• Peter Zachariou
• Gareth Lowndes
• Kimberleigh Yeomans

left it too late, and as 185 went past me I did the only thing I could – grab the shotline and come to a sudden halt. I was at 186 meters. A new women's cave record. So far so good ... but it is hardly ever the descent that kills you.

The ascent went smoothly. It was long and I was cold (all to be expected) and then it was over. It was finally time to get out, only thing was I didn't want to. Oh, I wanted to be warm and dry and not have a dv in my mouth, I just didn't want to find out if I had gotten my decompression right. I was feeling fine at 3 meters, but once I came up I couldn't get back in the water if I bent. There was no real choice, it was time and out I came.

Instead of the six people I had left behind the place was packed with people, there were TV crews and cameras and the only thing I could think to say was "My feet are squishy." Hardly words that inspire (they were - I had not had access to a toilet for five hours and had been drinking energy drinks constantly). I was ecstatic. I had made it. And although it wasn't the all time world record, it was a new women's cave record. I came up with some more suitable quotes for the cameras and they left in a rush, trying to make the seven o'clock news. That left me with only one question, had Derek phoned my friends and family to tell them I was OK? There my team was, trying to get me out of my dry suit and into warm dry clothes and all I wanted to know was had someone phoned my mom and told her I had come back?

It didn't take long for the euphoria to wear off and reality to set in. I had to wait at least three hours before I could try and walk out. There is a strict rule on deep dives against physical exertion after the dive, which makes getting out of Boesmansgat a challenge - you have to do it without significantly raising your heart rate. After an hour, instead of starting to feel better, I started to feel worse. I couldn't breathe properly. Every time I got to the end of a breathe I wanted to cough. The rest of the team had moved off into the shade and opened celebratory drinks, leaving only Kim (my surface marshall) to look after me. We were good enough friends for her to realise that I wasn't OK.

The doc came over to take a look. "Don't worry," she said. "It's just too much oxygen, there's nothing wrong."

Which is around the time things got really scary.

I was lying down when it felt like someone was taking a hot laser and moving it slowly over my body, starting from the tips of my fingers and feet and moving toward my body. Today I know what this means - my tissues are on the verge of bubbling and I'm about to bend. Then, all I knew was that something wasn't right. I suspected I was close to bending and there wasn't a darn thing I could do about it. I was paying the price, not of bad dive planning, but of not being fit enough. Food poisoning had not helped matters either.

It took five hours before I could find the energy to leave the water and start the walk out. Scratch that, I never found the energy - I simply had no choice. There were two ways to get back home, I walked or they strapped me to a stretcher and carried me. No way I was I going to admit to being so badly off that I couldn't walk out, so walk I did, using every bottle of Energade I could get my hands on. It took almost an hour to get to the cars and the sun was already setting. I was exhausted and nauseous and feeling really, really horrid. But I didn't bend (not officially). I woke the next morning still exhausted, but otherwise fine.

Exhaustion is my one lasting memory of that dive. I could hardly move. I just had nothing left in my body, no energy reserves, nothing. But it just didn't matter, I was the deepest woman in a cave, finally!

As the fuss started to calm down I realised that nothing had changed - not really. I had set out on this quest mainly to change how it felt to be me and to all intents and purposes now that it was behind me, I was still the same scared and unsure person I had always been. Days passed and I started to notice that there a difference. When I walked into a room full of people who knew more than me I found that I had this thing that I had done, that was mine. I had faced fear so intense I thought it would consume me but I had survived. I had found my courage.

There was however the issue of the record. When I came out of my 186-meter dive, I was content. Thanks to the altitude at Boesmansgat I had the unofficial depth record and an official (if not recognised by Guinness) cave record but these were distinctions that only existed within the diving community. Guinness only recognises two world records for scuba diving - the all-time deepest dive by a woman and the all-time deepest dive by a man. This depth is numerical, being the highest number that a diver reaches as measured by a depth gauge or metered line. It does not matter if you are in a cave or at altitude, if you are on open circuit or a re-breather, if you want to make 'the book' you have to have the biggest number for your gender. Simple!

My desire had never been to dive deep in the ocean, it had been to dive deep in a cave, which I had done. After all, the record had not been really what it had been all about – had it? I was finding that being recognised by the small technical community didn't have the assurance I had expected. Yes, this was mine, but in my head I heard the whispers, "It is not a real record, it wasn't the deepest."

(4) This Time, it's for Real

After the stress and intensity of getting to 186 meters, I had made the conscious decision to leave the world of records behind me and start living a normal life, or at least one that was about more than diving. For almost a decade diving had been the only thing I was interested in and with the record behind me I began to realise the price I had paid. Without my obsession, my life was totally empty. I was totally disconnected from friends and family - in part a conscious decision as it meant that any guilt I might feel about something so selfish as a deep dive was non-existent. Now I wanted it all back. I wanted to have a social life, friends ... a boyfriend.

But I was bored. I missed the camaraderie of being in a dive team and the focus that an ambitious plan like breaking a record provided. Suddenly, going back and doing 220 meters didn't seem to be such a bad idea. After all, it should be easier second time round. Now I knew the risks. Now I knew how to do the dive. I was also no longer the newcomer without a reputation, all factors that should mean getting support would be a whole lot easier.

I started to toy with the idea of 220 meters and after gathering a couple of the divers from the last trip (Joseph Emmanuel, Peter Zachariou, Derek Hughes and John de Wet), we started to do build up dives. Almost immediately things started to go wrong. First, Peter Zachariou was in a bad car accident and declared medically unfit to dive for two years. Then Joseph came out from supporting one of my deep dives with a bad migraine, or so we thought. As the afternoon progressed the migraine didn't disappear. Instead, Joe started to get worse and worse, vomiting and getting belligerent when asked if he was OK (Joe never loses his temper, never mind gets grumpy). Finally, we gave him an ultimatum - unless he could tell us his name he was going to the hospital - even if we had to force him. He couldn't and we gently man handled him into the closest vehicle and drove him the 60 kilometers to the closest hospital.

No one got much sleep that night, waiting to find out if Joe was OK or not. You never really know whether or not you should force a diver to go to the hospital. What if it's nothing? On the other hand, could any of us have lived with ourselves if it was something serious and we made it worse by doing nothing? Turns out we were right to make him go. On arrival at the hospital he was transferred to the closest chamber where after two hours he began to get his memory back. We were immensely relieved. I doubt that I would have been able to make peace with myself if Joe had ended up with permanent brain damage as a result of one of my dives.

The good news was that there was no lasting damage. The bad news - he needed keyhole surgery to fix a hole in his heart. Whilst the doctors could not tell us whether or not it was in fact a cerebral bend, they did think that the fact that Joe had a patent foramina ovale (pfo or hole in his heart - we all have one as babies and for one in three of us it does not close over as it should) was significant and could have contributed to the entire incident. It seemed better to get the problem fixed even though it would mean that Joe wouldn't be diving for at least six months.

Which was a problem for my dive plans. It was early 2004 and I had set a final date for the official world record attempt at October. Without Joe I was starting to get really uneasy. Could I get that deep if not deeper a second time round? There is a saying that I heard somewhere along the line that has stuck with me: "Courage is not the absence of fear, it is instead the knowledge that there is something more important than fear." It was not that I did not have the courage, it was that I did not seem to have the same motivation that I had last time round. Going back and 'just' doing 'one more dive' wasn't turning out to be that easy. I was battling to find my commitment and as a result was finding any excuse to put off diving (the weather would be too rainy or cold, or I had a migraine or flu) a strategy that had managed to waste the rest of 2004.

I began to realise that my problem was not the planned 220 meter dive, it was my build up dive. One of the tricks I have for deep diving is to do one build-up dive (just before we take our three month winter break) that mimics my actual dive. The build-up dive carries the same decompression obligation as the deep dive (as we dive Badgat), but I have a better chance of surviving if something goes wrong as my access to rescue and medical resources is better. If I am successful on the build up I know that there is no real physiological reason for me to not make the actual dive. All in all a win-win situation.

My designated build up was 160 meters which meant I had to go back to the incline shaft, a dive I hated. Here I was, the deepest female cave diver in the world and I couldn't do a dive that was 20 meters shallower than my all time deepest. Yet, whenever I thought of going back into the incline I became overwhelmed by fear. The first time I tried, I reached the bottom of the main shaft but I was so uncomfortable that I never even started the three minute swim. I remember looking at the tunnel and then turning around … diving was supposed to be fun and I wasn't having fun, so I wasn't going on. I said nothing when I got out the water. Fear is not something you acknowledge publicly. I was supposed to be brave and invulnerable. Besides, voicing my fears would have only created doubt in my support divers and it was not like they could help me anyway. This time I didn't want to die, especially underwater and unless I got over this rather illogical fear it I would not get 220 meters. So I went back.

This time I managed to bully myself into getting to the actual shaft and even going in, but at 140 meters, the incline (which is already tight) gets even tighter. There was no way I could make myself go further. I turned around and got out the water - disgusted with myself. I had this strong sense of foreboding and no matter how hard I tried, I just couldn't rationalise away my fear of this dive. There was not much I could do to make the dive any safer either. My only real choice was to take a buddy along, but there was no one I could take. Joe was medically unable to dive and whilst Derek had stepped up and was now doing deep support, he was still too inexperienced to take into the incline. I wasn't prepared to risk a friend's life just because I could not get control of my mind which left me with only one choice, to get over it and dive solo.

Unable to concede (at least not to fear), I gathered the team together and we had one last go at re-working the plan in such a way as to give me enough of a feeling of security to get me to 160 meters and back. The biggest risk and my biggest fear was that something would go wrong while I was deep inside the incline shaft. From 160 meters it would take at least 10 minutes to get back to the main shaft which is where the majority of my support divers (read help) were waiting. Knowing the tightness of the incline I realised that if something went wrong at the back it would take time to solve. At depth, time means gas, so instead of the usual two extra cylinders I took an extra four cylinders - I would leave one at the bottom of the main shaft at 100 meters and carry on with three (and of course my twin set, making a total of 5 cylinders, almost 13,500litres of gas). Derek would carry spare gas as well and wait for me at the entrance to the incline rather than the bottom of the shaft. This would get me through the three minute swim to my first staged cylinder at the bottom of the shaft. If I ran out going up the shaft, my next staged cylinder would be at 30 meters but I would have to do a full 30 minutes of decompression before I could use it.

I now had a dive plan that was giving me a reasonable sense of safety, but I was still not sure if I would be able to force myself back into the incline. So I added more pressure; first a sponsor then a formal date for 220 meters. I was hoping all of this would make it that much harder to walk away just because I was petrified. It seemed doable and I found myself with a dive date of Easter with nothing left to do but get my mind around this dive.

A fear of death is not something that you can easily talk about. Firstly, the words are hard to come by - I could not explain it to myself, never mind other people. Secondly, the conversation makes most people extremely uncomfortable, so instead of being able to talk through my fears logically, I retreated into my head. Which is when I found an interesting book by the Dalai Lama, titled "How to Die and Live a Better Life". It proved to be the inspiration I needed.

The principle in the book was really simple: the one thing we can guarantee is that we will die, we just do not know when. If you accept that death is inevitable it makes no sense to live in fear of it. You cannot control your death, just your life, and the way you live it. The words connected. I would go back and see how far I got and if I did not make it this time then I would stop trying to get deeper.

Easter Sunday came (this time bright and sunny). The support divers were furiously getting ready as I waited in my car, trying to get my mind to calm down. It was a nice, warm summer's morning and the sound of Buddhist monks chanting blended seamlessly into the African bush (in a fit of boredom the year before, I thought high altitude walking sounded like fun and went off to see what Everest Base Camp looked like). I was feeling strangely calm. The monotony of the chanting was quieting that part of my brain that was panicking and I knew that this time I wouldn't turn around. I would either be alive in 6 hours, or not. I had no regrets. I had said my goodbyes. I started to walk down to the water accompanied by a dainty blue dragonfly. In the morning breeze a feather blew to my feet and I had the oddest feeling that these were signs that I was not alone. Everything would be OK!

It was time to dive.

The dive went according to plan and I made the incline with plenty of gas and time to spare. It was exactly as I remembered - tight, silty and isolated. I could feel the fear hovering on the edge of my consciousness. Forcibly I brought back the sounds of my Buddhist monks chanting, ignored the fear and went on, further and further into the incline. The restriction came into view and it looked as tight and scary as I remembered. The chant was drowning out the mounting fear and I carried on. Rather than just dropping (as I had been), I started to swim. I wanted this dive to be over so the sooner I got to 160 meters the better. It was then that it happened. One moment I was swimming, the next I was stationary.

I swore - as if I needed this! I only had so much time and so much gas to get to 160 meters and I couldn't afford to waste it here at 152 meters. I reached back to my fins. This was nothing more than my fin getting snagged on something (probably the line I was following). It wasn't unusual and took about four seconds to solve - all I had to do was reach back and unsnag the fin and then I could be on my way. I was more annoyed that I was wasting time and gas than worried. There was no way I could get out the water and tell everyone I had turned around just because I had freaked out over a snagged fin. I also wanted to be in clear water - the sudden stop had meant I had landed in the foot of silt at the bottom of the incline and had turned the water rust brown in a matter of seconds.

The visibility deteriorated rapidly as I struggled to reach my foot and the errant fin. My world had shrunk to a couple of centimeters. I was lost in a whirl of silt - red particles drifting furiously around me. My only reference now was the thin white line lying innocuously next to me. Thanks to the silt that little white line was going to be the only way I would be able to find my way out (ironically, it was also the reason I was stuck). After about 30-seconds it occurred to me that I wasn't yet free and that I was breathing too fast. The panic I had been keeping at bay had overtaken me and I finally realised that this was serious. This was no longer about getting free and then carrying on, this was about getting free and getting back alive.

I stopped everything. I had no time to waste, which meant I didn't have time to get this wrong. I did not know how long it would take to get free, which meant I had to make my gas last, which meant I *had* to stop breathing so fast. The realisation that this might be my last dive hit me … hard! I was going to die right there if I didn't make the right decisions. As I started to get control over my breathing I realised that I had known - somehow, I had known - that this dive would kill me.

There is an elegant simplicity to life and death situations. The whole world slows down and the only thing you have to focus on is staying alive. There was only one thing I had to worry about, getting moving again, which meant that there was no point in actually checking my gas supply or my time (both actions that I obsess about when I am deep). Either I got free or I ran out of gas and drowned. If I did manage to free myself, the fact that I had overstayed and my decompression plan was now useless would be a small price to pay – I would be alive - everything else was a problem to be solved later. If I was moving, I was alive and heading towards help - I would hold my breath if I had to but I would not die without a fight. Suddenly bending seemed a small price to pay to be alive and back on the surface.

I noticed that the fear that had plagued me on the surface was no longer there. I was calm - totally calm. I wasn't scared, which was odd - the thought of drowning underwater with no escape was my worst fear, yet here, it just seemed to be another option.

Time slowed even as it raced by. I thought of Derek. He would be waiting for me. I would be late; he would break his dive plan, coming into the incline, pushing past his 120 meter limit, hoping to find me. I could see the expressions on my friends' faces as the shallow support came swimming furiously out the cave with the slate that would say "Verna didn't come back". I could see the shock and pain, especially the pain. I could see my mother's face when she heard the news. I could hear her pain, feel her desolation. I had to find a way to live. I had to!

Right, so, what are my other options?

I had three: one; carry on doing what I was doing until I ran out of air. Two; cut the line. Three; remove my fin. The first was the easiest and would kill me. The second? Also easy, except for the fact that I would have loose line lying all around me which would create a very real risk of getting entangled all over again. Yet the third option, taking off my fin, hardly seemed better - I still had a three minute swim back to the main shaft and on one fin with almost no gas to breathe, it was going to be a hard ask.

Time was slipping by me and with it my gas. If I got free I would need to use my bc to lift me out, which meant I needed some gas left in my backmounts, so I switched over to my only full side slung. I was now well into my emergency plan (which is what it was for), and trying not to think about anything else going wrong (I had already used up my emergency plan, what would I use to manage another disaster?). In the back of my mind I was praying that the Scubapro dvs I was using really were the best. I was going to need every last breathe to get out of this one. If I got out.

Thanks to my dry suit and layers and layers of warm clothes I was battling to reach my fin. I finally managed to 'walk' my hand along my calf to my foot and reach my fin strap. I unclipped it (what a relief) and then the damn thing wouldn't come off.

"To hang with this!" I pulled my foot with all my strength. It worked and to my joy I was free.

"Yes!"

I turned ready to get the hell out of there, but realised that I had no idea if I had in actual fact turned the whole way round. In my excitement I had forgotten rule number one; never let go of the line. The next word that came into my head wasn't polite. I wasn't amused and gave myself a serious tongue-lashing. Now wasn't the time to make more mistakes. I was well overdue and had practically no gas left to breathe. Any minute now I was expecting to take a breath and get nothing. Luckily, I had already thought of how to get out of the incline in exactly that situation: because it was an incline, if I added air to my bc I would start to float, which would show me where 'out' was. Hardly elegant, because I would be bumping my head on the ceiling until I got out of the silt, but hey, I wasn't trying to get points for technique, I was trying to get out.

To my relief it worked. As I came out of the silt, I saw the line (my saviour and almost my death), lying to my left. I had turned properly after all. I moved over toward it and suddenly I was stuck, again! This was starting to get ridiculous. I was just not catching a break. All that hard work to get unstuck the first time and I was now right back where I started. This time it was one of my extra cylinders. I glanced down but really didn't have the time to sit and sort it out: I was almost out of gas. So I unclipped the cylinder. It was pretty empty having less than a quarter left, but I could not afford to throw gas away - it could be the difference between surviving an extra minute or not, so I grabbed a hose and dragged it along with me, like a balloon.

Two minutes later, I was at the top of the incline looking at a very worried Derek. With no time to explain, I signaled that I was OK and started the three minute swim with dread - not knowing if my gas would last and not knowing how long it would take with only one fin.

The next three minutes would officially be the longest of my life. It is hard, hard work swimming

Excerpts from 160m Dive Plan (Badgat)
• 17m (nine minutes); EAN 36
• 110m (20min); 10:65
• 165m (27min); 10:65
• 110m (34min); 10:65
• 80m; 70m; 60m; 55m
• 50m (54min); 10:65
• 36m (78min); EAN 36
• 12m (160min); EAN 36
• 6m (301min); oxygen

at 110 meters especially with one fin on. I had just spent over seven minutes at 152 meters under extreme stress and was battling to keep my breathing nice and slow. I was breathing too much and extremely worried that I would run out before I reached the spare cylinder just ahead of me. The only advantage was that I was no longer alone, which actually made me try harder. This was my problem and I would sort it myself before I placed Derek's life at risk.

Then, there it was - my spare cylinder. Of the four cylinders I had with me, all were well less than a quarter full (read a couple of minutes at most before I ran out of gas totally). I grabbed my stage with relief and started my ascent. I was alive but it was not over yet. All I had was a single cylinder to do over 30 minutes of diving that would normally require at least two cylinders, on top of which my breathing was way out of control so I was using more gas than usual. I was still too deep and at these depths every breath was simply taking too much of the gas I didn't have. I needed to get shallower faster and to do that I was going to have to remove decompression stops.

Now ordinarily the last thing you do is remove decompression stops (that is a sure fire recipe to bend and at sub-30 meters that generally means death). But, (unlike a lot of deep divers) decompression does not scare me so I do not plan my dives to get out of the water fast - I plan them to get out of the water safe, so I add extra decompression, especially at depth.

This strategy was based on numerous chats with diving doctors trying to find some nugget of advice that would give me an edge and limit my decompression risk. The only advice they ever gave was that the only way to prevent bending was to avoid getting bubbles in your blood in the first place. Standard decompression profiles don't focus on preventing bubbles formation. Instead, they focus on removing these 'silent' bubbles from 30 meters and shallower. Research had indicated bubble formation could be prevented by adding extra decompression stops into the profile at depth. I had followed this advice and added an extra 20 minutes into my deep ascent, but now I was faced with a real dilemma, I did not have enough gas to do the planned stops between 100 meters and 30 meters - I would have to cut out some of these deep stops.

I had another problem - my decompression schedule was based on staying only a certain amount of time at depth and whilst I had not been as deep as planned, I had stayed deep for way longer. This meant that I had far more helium in my system than my decompression schedule was designed to remove. My safety factor was the very deep stops I now could not afford to take.

So I compromised. Based on my deco schedule my danger spot had been 50 meters. I cut every other stop down to a minute or less and got to 50 meters as fast as I could. I then sat, and sat, and sat, doing almost 15 minutes of decompression on a cylinder that got emptier and emptier. Did I say that the three minute swim was the longest of my life? Well, sitting at 50 meters just watching my cylinder get emptier and emptier must have been the second longest. I was using every trick in the book to slow my breathing down and I was still using too much gas.

Just 20 meters above me lay all the gas I could breathe. Only I couldn't use it, not until I had done this stop. Once again, I felt the panic start to take hold. I have been deep once before and run out of gas and it wasn't a pleasant feeling. You never know if you will make be able to hold your breath long enough to get to your next cylinder. I had worked so hard to get to this point and I was so close to surviving this dive. I knew that if I bolted from 50 meters and grabbed my next cylinder I would in all probability bend, and it wouldn't be a small bend: not with what I had just done. I forced myself to stay put, telling myself that I would stay until I had nothing left to breathe, only then would I bolt to 30 meters. It seemed silly to waste all that time and effort getting to this point only to kill myself because I couldn't wait ten minutes. I also knew the more deco I managed to get in, the better my chances of not bending.

Support divers came and went, each looking immensely relieved to see me. They told me afterwards that I was quite a sight to see, covered in silt, with a piece of fencing attached to my cylinders, and only one fin. My one-liner on a slate didn't do much to quench their curiosity - "Got stuck on line, had to leave fin behind". Gareth arrived, shook my hand and gave me his fin. Thank heaven. After my short three minute swim with one fin I wasn't looking forward to the eight minute one still ahead of me.

Sitting there in the blackness of the main shaft, listening to the sound of my heart beating and watching the support divers, the dive finally caught up with me and I started to cry. There was no way I could stop it. I felt such intense relief and gratitude. I remembered the feather and the dragonfly and realised I had not been alone down there. I had made it back and I knew that my world record would no longer be a problem. I would make it just fine. I was alive and I was no longer afraid.

All things considered, the dive went amazingly well. I didn't get any symptoms of a major bend. My only problems started when I got onto pure oxygen at six meters. It took barely ten minutes before I started to feel sick. Not a good sign considering I had almost two hours to go before I could surface.

By the time I did surface I wasn't feeling well at all, totally nauseous with no energy. It had been a fight to stay in the water for all of my oxygen decompression and as I lay on the surface I burst into tears. Derek was watching me closely, trying to work out what was wrong. I had no pain, but was I bending? I remember him saying over and over and over, "V, you have to tell me what's wrong. What do we tell the doctors?" I had no clue what was wrong, which was more frightening than being stuck. All I could do was tell them I wasn't feeling well and then throw up.

Now the normal protocol for a diver who comes out of the water after a deep dive and is not feeling well is to put them onto oxygen. My problem *was* the oxygen. I spent a good ten minutes fighting with support divers refusing another breath of oxygen. Around me, other dive teams were coming and going, curiously looking on. Everyone knew who I was and everyone was paying attention. I no longer cared what this all looked like. I wasn't feeling well, I was tired and I had just almost died.

After a while I started to feel better, but the doctors wanted get me to the closest hospital for a check up. I wasn't arguing, which is always a sure sign that I need medical attention. My blood pressure was low, way low, and I could hardly stand without getting lightheaded. Derek and his fiancée rushed me the 60-odd kilometers over the mountain pass to the hospital. I arrived without a phone or money and without any argument agreed to an overnight stay in high care. Which came as a surprise to everyone (including the consulting doctor) who all thought I would put up a fight, but I was feeling so bad and scared that I figured the last thing I needed was to ignore medical advice and then end up bending badly in the night an hour away from help.

When Sunday dawned, I was back to my old self. The verdict? Dehydration, low blood pressure and slightly burnt lungs from overexposure to oxygen. I was released and gladly went home to spend the day with my family. I never did tell them how close I had come.

The Curve Ball

With the build up out of the way all that remained was a dry period of intensive gym before the actual dive. I had four months to get back in shape and then a world record to set. Normally the only thing that I had to deal with during this 'rest' period is my mind. Then, on a Wednesday that I will never forget, I got a phone call telling me my mother had not made it to work, that her car was still in the garage, the house all locked up and no answer from inside.

It took me ten minutes to do a drive that normally takes thirty. We had to break her back door down to find her, unconscious, in her bathroom. She had been there, alone and helpless since the night before. An ambulance was called and she was rushed off to hospital. Did I say the three minutes in the shaft were the longest in my life?

It was June: my mother and I were three days away from a two-week holiday that we were both looking forward to, and instead I was sitting in a hospital listening to the doctor tell my brother and I that she needed emergency surgery to remove a pool of blood on her brain or she would die.

A couple of days later, just when it was supposed to get better, just when my mother was regaining consciousness, there was an incident with her ventilator - she went without oxygen for an extended period of time. She never recovered and, even though we refused to believe it, the doctors believed her to be brain dead.

This was the most important person in my life, my anchor. I was standing, every day, holding her hand, watching a person I didn't recognise talking to someone who couldn't hear, trying to work out what to do. What was it I was supposed to do? How was I supposed to deal with this? How?

In the early hours of a cold July morning I got a phone call from the hospital telling me to come. It was a week before her birthday. "You need to come," a voice told me. "The doctors say you must come." The sun had not yet risen and in the cold of the early morning I calmly started my day – a day I knew I would not want to ever commemorate. I tried to get hold of my brother, but there was no answer. I got up, got into the shower, got dressed and went to the hospital. I was there, holding my mothers hand, when she died.

It had taken a little over six weeks. I had never gotten around to telling her about the time I almost died. How I wish I had!

With my mom's death behind me, the world started again. I was supposed to be doing a deep dive in six weeks' time. In the vacumn and sheer desolation that her death brought, the only thing that I had was that dive. She had been so proud of me, so excited that I was going back. I couldn't let her down.

There was no way I would make October, so we changed dates to November and I threw myself into preparing for the dive.

With my mother's death, everything changed. Whilst I no longer had to worry about disappointing her or causing her grief, I had a new worry - my three year old niece, Michaela. Michaela and my mom had been almost inseparable and she was battling to come to terms with her granny's sudden disappearance. I guess I stepped into the vacumn my mother left behind. It is easy for me to justify dying and leaving adults behind to cope. Coping is what adults do - besides, I cannot control how a single person out there sees the world or chooses to experience it. I cannot make anyone happy or sad - those are choices that they have to make for themselves. But children; children are different. They are still learning and there was no way I could justify the effect my dying would have on Michaela. I couldn't cause her that much pain.

Simply put, I knew that I wouldn't be able to push this dive as I had before. I knew that I would turn around rather than risk dying. Which is the right frame of mind if you want to live but not the right frame of mind if you want to achieve a record: the whole point of records is that you have to push past not only your own comfort zone, but also that of the world. You have to risk your life, yet now, risking my life wasn't a price I wished to pay.

Getting Going

I kept all the doubt to myself and focused instead on Nov 25th. Much to my surprise the team conflict that I had experienced doing 186 meters was starting to reappear. Which was odd as I had made a concerted effort this time to choose team members who were personal friends, so there should not have been personal agendas.

The first problem was the introduction of girlfriends. My strongest supporter Derek had started a relationship that was to turn into marriage and a family of his own. The problem was that we were diving every other weekend, which wasn't conducive to a relationship, especially a new one. In an effort to accommodate this new important person in his life I broke my cardinal rule – I let girlfriends join us on our deep diving weekends. The result was catastrophic.

Watching the reaction of an outsider to our diving was nerve-wracking. I was suddenly diving in an emotional whirlwind, which was more than I could handle. Diving was supposed to be a place of peace where I could escape. Instead, it became a battleground. If we didn't phone in after a dive, all hell broke lose. Every decision, every action was questioned. Were we being safe? It was bad enough trying to get over my mother's death. There was no way I could cope with the emotions that were now infecting every weekend. I reinstated the no-girlfriend rule across the board.

Which went down like the Titanic. Derek was given a choice - he could dive or he could have his relationship, but not both. I was given the choice, either lose Derek as a team member or allow his fiancée to come to Boesmansgat. We were a month away from the dive and I was now embroiled in a power struggle I didn't need and certainly wasn't expecting.

I didn't want to lose Derek on the dive - he was one of the people I trusted and relied on. But, when I visualised the trip with emotionally invested people who didn't understand what it was we were doing, it made me want to throw up. No matter which way I looked at the dilemma, my gut was telling me that I needed to keep this dive an emotion-free zone. I could barely cope with the emotional load I was already carrying and I did not want to be reminded on a daily basis once on the trip of the fear and the uncertainty that comes hand in hand with a record. No one did!

I was also tired, very, very tired. The effect of losing my mom meant that I had little patience for the world around me. I certainly didn't have enough energy to be sucked any further into another drama. I didn't know how I would manage the dive without Derek, but so be it! I let go and walked away. At the end of the day it boiled down to the fact that, no matter what, this dive was about my life and no one else's, and I had to make decisions that worked for me, not decisions that worked for other people. This was about me, no one else. It had to be.

I remember the conversation with Derek clearly. We were at an impasse and we both knew it. I wasn't willing to change my mind, even though I knew it meant losing Derek as a friend never mind on the dive. He - rightly - placed his relationship above the dive and so couldn't go on the trip if his fiancée couldn't accompany him.

I was losing my friend over a dive. Should I have conceded? I still wonder.

The closer we got to the trip, the more things started to go wrong. My distraction meant that I had (once again) not proactively taken command of the dive team. This left the door open (once again) for various members to try and take control. A situation I didn't notice until it was too late.

Because of the extreme nature of a dive like this, I like having people around me who second guess me. I am not looking for 'yes' men. But I have yet to find a way of making it work without the conflict and inevitable lost friendships. Leadership sounds so easy when you read about it in books and if I ever do another deep dive it will be to see if I can get this one point right.

As the dive got closer, my insecurity started to increase which was making everything harder. I was plagued by doubts and finding it harder than usual to accept constructive criticism. Ordinarily, I would end up getting defensive, the situations would get confrontational and I would just abdicate. This time I was trying to change the pattern but I was having to work hard at listening to the comments of the people around me and not just shut them out. It would have been far easier to just shut everyone out and treat their comments as personal insults to my competence and ability. The thing was I knew my life depended on my dive plan, so I had no choice - if I wanted the best dive plan I could get, I needed their input.

Having a team that knows diving and can challenge my plan has always been a part of my edge. No matter how long I do this or how many dives I get, there is no way that I as a single individual can think of everything. On top of that, the way I see the dive and the way others see the dive are different. We focus on different things. The more people who scrutinise the plan, the better the chances that we will find the gaps before I am on the dive, and the more issues we solve out of the water, the more chance I have under the water.

I battled on, missing having Derek on board to filter all of this extra drama. Then, at the last minute, Derek announced he was back on the team. I could have kissed his fiancée. I am not sure that she knew how grateful I was that she was able to get to a place where it was OK for Derek to be on the team without her. I do know how hard it was for her; even if that would never be something we would talk about. I now had Derek's management skills back and could focus my attention away from the team and back on getting my body and mind where they needed to be.

I had been expecting to go through the same paralysing fear I had experienced in 2001, but as the dive started to get closer, I was still fear free. I was unsure if that was because I was still numb from my mom's death or if it was true intuition. For the first time on a dive that pushed my own limits, I was calm when thinking about the dive. It would be what it would be. I couldn't predict it, I could only prepare for it and then trust.

Finally, it was the night before we were to leave Johannesburg. It had been a hectic six weeks trying to pull together the logistics, which on an expedition like this, are formidable. To avoid the near-disaster we had last time when the gas almost did not arrive, we were taking all our own helium and oxygen with us. Think five oxygen cylinders and eight helium cylinders - each almost 2m high with a combined weight of three tons and you start to understand our dilemma. Now add two compressors, 15 stage cylinders plus personal dive kit and you simply don't have enough vehicles to get everything to Boesmansgat. Luckily, we were loaned a Volkswagen panel van (by Volkswagen) which comfortably fitted all the bulky, heavy kit, leaving the private vehicles to pack up everything else.

Having done as much up front prep as we could, all that remained was the final packing – which we were going to do at Derek's house. The plan was to meet at Derek's, pack the van and then rush home to get our own packing done before leaving in the morning. The helium and oxygen had been delivered the week before and all that was left was for Gareth to arrive with the 15 cylinders and compressors that WUC was loaning us. Two hours after Gareth was supposed to arrive Joseph received the phone call notifying us that there would be no compressors or cylinders. Gareth had not asked the WUC committee for permission and they were refusing to release the kit.

What patience I had evaporated instantaneously. I wasn't sure whom I was more angry with - Gareth for not asking for permission or the committee for choosing the night before we were leaving to play politics. It took hours on the phone to resolve, but finally, looking sheepish, Gareth arrived with the kit. I breathed a huge sigh of relief when we finally closed the door on the van.

600 kilometers later and we were finally back at Boesmansgat and I started to relax. Most of the team had been on

the last trip, so everyone knew what needed to be done. The dive itself was (in theory at least) an easy jump: all I was doing was going from 186 meters to 221 meters, only 40 meters deeper. I told myself I wasn't doing anything new: the men had been as deep (and deeper) and survived.

I tried to ignore the fact that you never know until it is too late if you are going to make it or not. You never know if your planning is adequate until you do the dive and what makes it worse is that there is no one in the world to ask.

Even though I was calm and unconcerned about the outcome of the dive, I was still obsessing about it. Yes, there had been divers who had made it as deep and survived. There had also been divers who I deem to be far greater than I, who have attempted these depths, supremely confident and super fit, only to never come back. Worse, they came back badly bent if not paralysed with permanent physiological damage (loss of short term memory, loss of hearing, loss of balance). I was not prepared to pay for a dive with my life or my hearing. Just because you are no longer able to count the number of people who have dived below 200m on two hands does not mean that it has become a safe dive.

And there was still this question hanging over me - was I going to be able to explore my own personal unknown?

Getting to the Water is Harder Than Diving

So far this had been an unusual build up for a trip as I was not plagued by paralysing angst and fear. The calm with which I had walked out of Badgat was still there and I was finding it impossible to stress about the outcome of the dive. My focus was on getting through the next couple of days without coming down with the now infamous Boesmansgat lurgy. Last time it had taken only a day for me to succumb. This time it took three.

We were well on track and things were going relatively smoothly. The team was holding together and I was congratulating myself on not getting ill. So far no one had, which made us think our strategy of not drinking the water had worked. No one knew why, but normally within a day or two at Boesmansgat, the entire dive team comes down with bad diarrhea and vomiting. We had decided it was the water (and not the venison which was one of the perks of staying at the

The Team:
• Derek Hughes
• Joseph Emmanuel
• John de Wet
• Allana Barber
• Ian Gatley
• Kirsten Emmanuel
• Gareth Lowndes
• Theo van Heerden
• Gordon Hiles
• Don Shirley
• Dave Shaw

farm), but at six meters the precursor to the lurgy, nausea, finally struck. I managed to finish my dive and get back to my room before I started the inevitable vomiting. When the rest of the team arrived back for supper the paramedics were sent in and I got given the option of the needle or tablets. I didn't care, so long as the nausea and vomiting stopped. It took two pills and another two days for me to recover. I was hoping that the fact that I was immediately treated coupled with three months of intense cardio training had given me enough fitness absorb these two days of illness and still have enough left to get me through the dive ahead.

Even though I was in bed, the trip was moving forward with Derek at the helm. Every evening the team would meet to discuss what had happened during the day and what had to be done tomorrow. With little time, we had to keep to the daily schedules and do whatever it took to meet the milestones, the two most important being getting the shotlines in and the stage cylinders set. I did not expect everything to go smoothly and knew that we would have to prioritise carefully to make sure we were focusing on the right things. I was not overly concerned about missing these evening sessions as I was expecting Derek to liaise closely with me, especially when it came to sorting out delays and making choices about what we would or would not sacrifice in order to make our schedule. Instead, the trip started to take a direction of Derek's choosing and I found myself with no input at all. I began to get a sickening feeling of déjà vu. Somehow I had once again managed to lose control of my own trip.

It was extremely frustrating! I knew how to dive yet getting to the dive was dependant on getting the dive team headed in the right direction and that was the bit I just could not seem to get right. I didn't even know what had gone wrong or how I had arrived at this point. What made it harder was that the person who had betrayed me was Derek. I was supposed to be able to trust him and count on him. It was my trip, it was my dive and it was my life. I had not given him the authority to take control of my trip and make decisions on his own. The decisions were mine to make; I was the one who paid the price if they were wrong.

I resigned myself to the fact that the chances of me being able to get control back without burning bridges were slim and just did the best I could which is a strategy I hate, because the best I could do wouldn't be good enough. I knew that I would have to challenge Derek at our daily meetings and I knew that doing so would destroy our friendship. I placed the consequences firmly in the 'for after the dive' category and got on with it. The first meeting I attended was not pretty. I was actively participating and my decisions directly contradicted Derek's. We moved on, now with an underlying unease and tension that would last well after the trip had ended. Whilst we may no longer have liked each other much, no one was giving up and going home. We had a record to break.

My first concern was whether or not I was still fit enough, so I dragged Kirsten (Joe's wife, close friend and surface marshall) mountain biking. To my relief, we managed the 18 kilometer round trip to the hole and back just fine. With that worry out of the way we were now officially all systems go for the deep dive.

During my bout with the dreaded lurgy both Don Shirley and Dave Shaw had arrived and with their arrival our team was finally complete. I had never met Dave but he had come highly recommended by Don. As for Don, we had never dived together but as the resident technical diving 'professional' his reputation preceded him. Together Don and Dave had been getting noticed in diving circles, doing some impressive exploration with a dive to 186 meters at Badgat (the official back of the incline shaft) and then 220 meters at Boesmansgat - which gave Dave an unofficial world record for depth on a re-breather.

When Don heard that I would be going back for the all time record he had volunteered to mix gas for us and do the deeper support dives. As Dave had already been to 220 meters it made a whole lot of sense to have them both on the team. It meant that if something went wrong at 220 meters there would be someone close by who could come down and help. It was an immense relief and what little worry I had been experiencing evaporated. If I couldn't solve the problem myself I wasn't dead, all I had to do was hold out until Dave arrived. Dave however was not there just to be a support diver. He was back to see if he could get past Nuno's cave record of 282 meters and was planning on using my dive as his deep build up to stage cylinders for his deeper push a couple of days later.

The week before D-day is always hectic and this trip was no different. With the late arrival of Don and Dave we had to fit in two 150 meter build up dives for Don and Dave as well as get all the filling done, cylinders tested and then placed on the line. The line had turned out to be quite a job to get in place, especially as we had not one, but two lines to install. The first would hold my stage cylinders and of course the white tag that that would indicate 220 meters. As we wanted this dive to be acknowledged as an official world record we were doing as much as we could to prove that I had in fact reached my depth. The tag was to be my proof and to prevent me just taking a copy with me, going to 100 meters and then coming back, we had it signed by Andries and Debby (the farmer and his wife), attached to the line in front of witnesses and then immediately dropped to 220 meters. The only way we were going to get it back was by me fetching it or us bringing up the line.

Alongside this main shotline was another line that I would descend on. It did not have stage cylinders clipped to it, so I would not have to keep on letting go of the line and then getting back onto it in order to avoid cylinders - an issue that I felt would slow me down considerably. With the lines installed and the stage cylinders finally in place (and checked by myself) we were ready to do *the* dive. We took a day off to recover and relax and then it was time.

Deepest, Finally!

We had spent a large amount of time the night before going over the dive plan to make sure that everyone knew when they had to get into the water and what they were supposed to do when they were underwater. I didn't want anyone living out the rest of their lives thinking it was their fault or that they should have done something better, so we spent some time outlining what they were supposed to do if something went wrong.

All that was left was the dive. Our six am start was early for me, but as we were not camping at the hole (instead choosing the comfort of the game lodge nine kilometers away) we had a 20 minute drive ahead of us to get to the site, followed by the walk in. My dive was planned for just over five and a half hours and I wanted to make sure that if I did bend, there was plenty of daylight to manage the situation and if necessary, have me flown out, which meant I had to get into the water by nine. I figured three hours was more than enough to get everyone going and ready.

No one wanted to be late so people started moving early, which meant even though I only needed to get up at six, I was awake much earlier. Not that I needed or even wanted to have more time before the dive. When I wake up all I want to do is get in my car and go diving, I do not want to eat or chat. However, the rest of the team does not suffer the same attack of nerves and breakfast is always a jolly affair. Underneath everyone knows that this might be the last real meal for a while, especially if something goes wrong.

I avoided breakfast (there was no way my stomach would accept food and I didn't want to talk to anyone) and instead tried to find a space where no one could find me until it was time to get into the vehicles and move off to the hole. I definitely wanted to avoid the rest of the team as much as I could. Whilst I was comfortable with the risks on this dive, I didn't want to be surprised by visible signs of concern or fear in the people around me. I didn't want to think about the consequences and I certainly did not want to start the dive with new doubts. I definitely didn't want to talk about it, all of which made for an uncomfortable start to the day. No one really knew what to say or do and no one wanted to distract me or make me start doubting myself. The space around me grew and as I started to get my mind where it needed to be.

Finally, breakfast was over and the team started to make their way to their cars. I was already in mine, listening to the now familiar sound of my Buddhist monks chanting. First one vehicle started and moved out, followed by another and another. I slipped into the convoy and we started the 20 minute drive to the hole in the pre-dawn light.

The drive is always strange. The sun is barely at the horizon and the Karoo is quietly alive, fresh and crisp. Colours jump out at me and I seem to notice every detail, the patterns and textures of the bush, the cautious glances of the herds of buck, the calls of birds. I always end up wondering whether or not I would be the one driving back again later. Would there be a later? I glanced over to the picture of my mother and niece to remind myself why there had to be a later and carried on to the hole, now in no great hurry.

I arrived at the hole to see the last of the support divers starting down the slope. I needed to give them about 15 minutes to get sorted at the bottom before I got there, so I just sat and waited. My mind was well into the dive and to all intents and purposes the world was no longer there.

Once I was at the hole things became slow and methodical. This is a well rehearsed sequence of events, almost a ritual. First I attach my dvs to my twin set and check that everything is OK. Then I strip down to my bikini and get into a layer of thermals and underwear to keep me warm. Finally I squeeze into my dry suit and then slip into the water to begin getting into the layers of kit.

Basic Configuration

- Twin 15 litre steel cylinders with isolation manifold (dived closed)

- Two independent ScubaPro Wings

- Dive rite harness and locally produced metal back place (yes, I have a buckle on my harness)

- Locally produced canister torch

- Helmet with two Scubapro pocket lights

- Back mounted dvs – Two ScubaPro X650's with MK25 first stages. Both with spgs

- Side slungs (four 10l aluminum cylinders), with two Scubapro S600s, One Scubapro R390 and one Poseidon Cyklon 5000 (on my absolute last resort backup cylinder)

As I asked for it, kit was passed over. Gareth was checking to see that everything was secured properly and I could reach everything, sorting out any hose tangles that might arise. All around me, the rest of the team stood in various stages of readiness. Don and Dave were already in the water, quietly waiting. They would be the first divers down after me and rather than be late had opted to wait the 10 minutes in the water.

As for me, I am partly there and partly already in my head and on the dive. I remember only the sense of purpose and hushed quiet before the dive. I know that everyone is watching, making sure that everything goes on right, that I do not make any mistakes.

With all my kit attached there are only my final checks to go and true to form, I discover that my torch is not working (something always goes wrong, and at least this was a small thing). A mad scramble located a spare bulb … and then there was nothing left to do but dive.

With a brief "See you later" I started my descent. (I know - I should try for something a bit more impressive as my 'last' words, but what else is there to say? Anything else would be pretentious).

Even though the fear had not arrived, my nerves were in full swing and the adrenaline was pumping. Since waking I had been running my mantra through my head trying to keep my analytical mind busy somewhere else. I needed to be focused on the dive, on what must be done and not obsessing about what could go wrong. It is an odd frame of mind. There's the 'me' that focuses on what I'm doing and then there's a more distant 'me' that observes what's happening. As I reached the ceiling at 40 meters the observing part of me noticed that I was having fun: this was what it was supped to be like underwater.

Things were going well. I was rapidly picking up momentum, which was good news – it meant I would get to 221 meters in time. As I slipped under the ceiling the lights of the camera above me faded. Now it was just me, the dark, my bubbles and the clack, clack of the line as I slipped ever down.

I reached 150 meters and switched from the side slung cylinder I was breathing to the two cylinders on my back. This was part of my strategy to ensure that all I was doing when I got to 221 meters was reaching for my tag and not worrying about swapping cylinders or running out of gas to breathe.

The other part of my strategy was to give myself a number of exit points. I was really concerned that I no longer had the commitment to make it to 220 meters and that I would chicken out well short of my mark. By giving myself a number of options I didn't have to focus on one huge, intimidating number (221 meters) and I was hoping that as I reached each of the easier milestones it would be easier and easier to convince myself not to waste the time I had already spent in the water and carry on to the next milestone instead. If I was lucky, before I knew it I would be looking at my tag. Even though I knew it was a trick, it always worked - I could get myself to do things so long as my mind was under the impression that it could leave at any time. After that, finding reasons to stay was pretty simple.

My first milestone was 186 meters – which sounded doable since it was a dive I had done before. I figured even a meter deeper than that would save my honour and reputation and I could turn around. If I was feeling good then I would carry on to 200 meters, because, well, it was 200 meters. If things were still going well I would move my sights to 211 meters which was the current all time record. If push came to shove, I could turn around at 212 meters with a new record: hardly an impressive way to break a record, but it would still be broken. Every meter after that was a bonus, and my tag sitting at 221 meters? Well, that was the real prize and if I had made it that far, realistically within reach.

Before I knew it, I was at 187 meters. I was surprised and quickly checked to see if I was getting any signals to turn. I had plenty of time left and as importantly, I was hardly using gas. I didn't even slow down, instead I carried on towards 200 meters.

Sometimes time goes slowly underwater and sometimes it seems to just fly past. Before I knew it, I was looking at my 200-meter marker. I breathed a sigh of relief and started to slow down, readying myself for 211 meters and then 221 meters. Slowing down was important. I couldn't reach 221 meters falling like a brick as below me would be 40 meters of nothing. I needed to glide to my tag and not have to grab onto the line to stop (which may have broken the shotline). I hit the brakes, pushing as much air into my bcs as I could to slow me down as fast as I could.

212 meters came and went and there seemed to be no reason to stop. No fear, no dread, plenty of gas to breathe and plenty of time. Seconds later I was at the ubiquitous tag that meant I was the deepest woman in the world. I glided to a stop, level with the tag and gingerly reached out to unclip it. This was the part of the dive that made me uncomfortable. In order to get the tag I had

to let go of the line I had used to descend and reach across a meter to the main shotline on which the tag was attached. I would, however briefly, be suspended in the middle of nowhere no reference points other than the lines. If I didn't have perfect control when I let go and moved to the other line I could find myself losing both lines, and if I lost a line the chances were not good that I would ever be able to find my way back.

As I leaned over to get the tag I noticed a slight shake in my hands and put it down to nerves. My heart was still pounding even though I was calm and in control. To all intents and purposes my dive was done but as I was still having fun I decided not to just turn around and leave, but to take a minute and have a look around. I checked to see how much gas I had used (hardly any) and how much time I had left. To my surprise I was three minutes early. I didn't want to get overconfident and make a mistake now (not with five and a half hours ahead of me before I could even start to consider the dive successful). I gave myself a minute, and just experienced where I was. Even my powerful torch didn't seem able to penetrate the inky blackness that surrounded me. Slowly pirouetting around the thin, white line I realised I was completely alone, no fish, no life, no light, no walls - only the sound of my bubbles and heartbeat. It was truly awesome. I couldn't even see the bottom (which couldn't have been more than 30 meters below me). I turned and looked back up the line, but all I could see were two faint specs of light - Dave and Don coming under the ceiling to meet me.

And then I left.

As I made my way to my first decompression stop at 150 meters Dave and Don's lights got brighter and brighter. It was a strange sensation. There was no noise - something I had always equated with company underwater. Instead, they glided effortlessly and silently through the water on their re-breathers. I waved my tag at them. Dave gave me a cheery OK and continued down to 180 meters to set his deep stages for his push in two days. Don turned, looking equally pleased, and together we carried on up the line. I was enjoying myself immensely.

The ascent is really the hard part of a deep dive. It had taken twelve minutes to get to 221 meters and now it would take over five hours to get out of the water. Whilst I had made the depth there were still a couple of places where things could go wrong, especially when I got close to 50 meters. This seems to be the danger point, when you change mixes and re-introduce nitrogen into your system, and historically seemed to be the point at which deep water bends occurred. There was also the not-insignificant chance that a piece of equipment failed which could mean losing part or all of the gas I was carrying with me. I wasn't really worried about that - I would have to hold my breath to reach spare gas, but there was plenty of that above me. I was worried about bending underwater. That would be far harder to manage.

As the dive progressed I slowly got shallower and shallower, meeting more and more of my support team. My decompression was carefully planned to provide lots of shorter stops in the ten to twenty minute range and so offset the boredom of the longer stops that were to come. Support divers came and went, huge grins on their faces when they realised I had made it. Camera's came and went, as did 50 meters, with no problems. However, time didn't come and go quite so quickly. With three hours to go I started to get cold which was when I discovered that the next three hours would be really uncomfortable; the heater I had installed in my dry suit was unplugged and there was no way to reconnect it.

In order to prevent getting bent I was drinking copiously. The downside was of course, that I now had a full bladder. Not a problem - I had on incontinence nappies for this very reason. I hate wearing nappies and getting wet and icky as a result, so had avoided doing a run-up dive that included using the nappy, completely forgetting that it took practice to undo years of learning – you do not go to the toilet when wearing clothes. I started to worry whether this was mental or physical, because an inability to urinate was a sign of decompression sickness. If I couldn't get this right, I was looking at a burst bladder and three hours before I could get to the surface. To my relief, the dam broke. I was warm - for about five minutes. Then the cold set back in. With an ambient temperature of 18 °C staying warm was hard. By the time I made my oxygen stop at six meters I was well chilled and starting to shiver.

Six meters is not a good spot to start shivering; it makes support divers nervous because they assume I am having oxygen convulsions and forget I might just be cold and hypothermic. This meant that I was regularly getting asked if I was OK, which was annoying. All I wanted was to stop thinking. I definitely didn't want to be woken up - every time that happened my mind remembered it was uncomfortable, cold and hungry and I would then have to spend the next five to ten minutes switching back off and not focusing on minutes that felt like hours.

And it is always the hours I have to spend at six meters that are the hardest. By now the novelty has worn off and you are seriously questioning the sanity of spending hours in the water for a silly label. All I wanted was get out of the water and get warm in the sun, with something to eat. Time crawled by! I was trying not to focus on the minutes in an effort to make things go faster, but it wasn't working. I had to pay attention to the time because I had to take breaks from the oxygen every 25 minutes. These oxygen breaks were standard practice and allow your lungs some time to recover from the pure oxygen, and as I had battled with the oxygen on my last dive, I was not going to eliminate them just to be more comfortable. In a last-ditch attempt to make things bearable I resorted to counting breaths rather than minutes. I worked out that I was taking two to three breaths a minute, which meant ten minutes was 20 breaths. I rarely made it, mostly getting to twenty breaths and only having wasted five or so minutes, but it passed the time.

There is no way to jazz up decompression. It is simply tedious. It is also the price you pay for depth. Mostly I just switch off and endure. Whenever I start to do something my mind starts to wake up and notice that I am wet, cold, hungry and uncomfortable, so I avoid waking up.

But decompression is not endless and without any sign of the bends my time was finally up. I surfaced with a huge grin on my face. I had made it and there were simply no words to describe what it felt like. My entire life had been about getting to that moment. This was the reward for all the fear, all the obstacles, all the frustration, tears and pain. I hoped my mother was proud of me.

All around me were grinning faces (and the inevitable reporters and TV crews). Not for the first time, I felt truly alive. I had reached the end of my journey and knew I would never be the same again.

(5) Raising the Dead

Whilst my part of the trip was over, there was still Dave's dive to see successfully done before we would be going home. I was particularly curious to see how another team would plan a dive that was looking to reach 300 meters, especially as they were going to be using re-breathers.

Re-breathers are controversial in diving and have a reputation for being unpredictable and therefore dangerous - especially at depth. They work on the principle of re-using a single breath of air, taking out the carbon dioxide in an exhaled breath and adding back oxygen, the management of which requires electronics. They also had never been below 220 meters without failing.

The first thing I noticed was the fact that neither Don nor Dave seemed to place the same value on support divers as I had. I consider competent, continuous support from 100 meters (if not deeper) as a key success factor to a deep dive, yet in their minds they were more than capable of managing any situation underwater and did not need assistance. Which was all well and good, but what happens when there is a problem that can't be solved? Surely then having a diver in the water to assist would be a necessity? Not having continuous support seemed like an unnecessary risk to take.

It was a good thing that they did not want continuous support because only Allana and Ian could stay on and whilst they were both competent divers, this was their first Boesmansgat trip and their exposure to deep diving was limited. Which meant that they did not have the required experience to be the only support on a dive as deep as the one Don and Dave were planning. To quiet my own concerns I volunteered to be surface marshall, which would mean there would at least be someone around who understood what was happening underwater should things go wrong. The paramedics were also able to stay on, which brought the team to five.

I think it was the day before Dave did his dive that he startled us at breakfast recalling a dream. He told us how he had dreamt of finding Deon Dreyer, face up in the mud on the bottom (Deon was a diver who had been lost on a shallow dive almost ten years previously). No one really took the dream seriously, not even

Dave. We forgot about it and focused on his dive plan. Which was relatively simple - Dave would descend on the shotline, then (using his own line), swim off to see how deep he could get. I recall him mentioning 300 meters as a target, but didn't think much of it (Nuno had battled to find 282 meters in 1996 and the water level had dropped considerably since).

Don would meet Dave at 180 meters on his ascent at 180 meters and was as deep as he could get on his machine without imploding the electronics. Even though Dave and Don were on re-breathers (and so needed little more than a single cylinder to do the dive), they had to plan for the very real risk that something would go wrong with a machine. If it did, the only way out would be using open circuit, which meant they still needed as many cylinders in the water as an open circuit diver would.

The dive itself promised to be pretty boring for those of us not diving. Dave would be gone for most of the day. I couldn't dive (even if I wanted to) and Allana and Ian would only be diving when the lads got to 30 meters. Their duties were restricted to popping in every hour to check if everything was still OK. I am not sure we really thought about what would happen if things weren't. There was really not much we could have done other than wait and see if Don or Dave could solve the problem themselves. If they couldn't, our job would be to make the phone calls notifying the world that they had not returned.

As always with deep dives, getting out of the water while it was still light was a challenge. In Dave's case he would be diving for over eight hours, which meant he needed to start the dive at six am. That translated to a four am start for the rest of us. With much yawning (and some halfhearted grumbling about the hour) we trundled off to the hole and watched as Don and Dave started to kit up. I have never seen two divers so self-sufficient. It was if we were only there to allay the concerns of the ever-critical diving community.

Without much ado Dave slipped under the water and began his descent. This was the signal for the rest of us. We now had seven minutes to get Don ready to descend. As Don started his preparation, his machine decided not to co-operate and we found ourselves with two machine failures in quick succession. No sooner did we fix one, then the next popped up. No one on the surface knew much about machines and with his machine not working, we were all expecting him to call the dive. Instead, with no time to spare we rushed around following Don's instructions trying to do last-minute repairs.

This reluctance to call the dive surprised us. Re-breathers are known for failing at depth. Don's dive was at the limits of his machine and if something went wrong with him at 180 meters, Dave wasn't going to be much help. Taking a machine that was failing before it even went into the water down to the very limit of what it can do just seemed far too risky, yet it just didn't cross

Don's mind to not do that dive. When we asked him if we needed to get him open circuit kit he shook his head furiously. He would rather go and do the dive with problems on the machine then switch to open circuit. He had more options, he said, on a machine than on open circuit. If he had to, he would run his machine manually (a level of task loading that surprised me), but he would be doing the dive and on his machine.

Finally, with seconds to spare, Don declared everything well and disappeared under the water. It was now out of our hands. We waited.

Waiting was why I normally do not volunteer to be support. It is far better to be the one in the water, there you know exactly what is going on. On the surface your mind starts to imagine all sorts of things. Finally, it was time for the first support diver to get in and find out what had happened. If Dave had made it deeper than 282 meters he would have broken Nuno's record and set an impressive new one for re-breathers. We were also worried about Don. Had his machine lasted?

The news that came back was surprising to say the least: both divers were fine, Don's machine had behaved and Dave had found Deon's body. I was stunned. I hadn't believed that anyone would ever find Deon. When he had disappeared almost ten years previously teams of divers and submersibles had been sent in to try and locate him and found nothing. He quite simply disappeared into the black vastness of Boesmansgat. What made it even more bizarre was that this meant that Dave's dream had come true. I couldn't wait until Dave surfaced to find out more.

There was no other excitement on the dive (thank heavens) and it was with anticipation that we helped Dave out of the water hours later. I can still hear his Aussie lilt as he told us "that finding Deon put paid to going deep." He had descended on the shotline as planned and then tied off his own reel when he reached the bottom. Once securely tied off (and now with a continuous line connecting him to the surface) he proceeded to swim off in search of depth. Instead, he came across Deon, lying exactly as he had dreamed; face up and cylinders stuck in the mud. Instead of continuing, he stopped and tried to retrieve him. Not an easy task for anyone to contemplate at 260 meters, especially on a machine.

Exertion has two effects on a diver, it increases the rate of breathing and so decreases the size of each breath. This combination of more shallow breaths means the body does not have time to take up oxygen and as importantly, get rid of carbon dioxide. Too much carbon dioxide and you pass out. To make matters worse, an increase in carbon dioxide increases your level of narcosis – you go from lucid to no longer able to think properly (and so identify the problem), to unconscious, to drowned in the space of minutes. On open circuit any carbon dioxide build up is easily managed by consciously slowing down your breathing and forcing air to remain in your lungs (and so take up oxygen and remove carbon dioxide), however machines are totally different beasts, especially at depth.

Two things work against re-breather divers at depth. Firstly, it takes more effort to breathe in and out, and secondly, the machine works by holding extra air in a number of air spaces. These extra air spaces must be regularly flushed which is normally achieved through the act of breathing in and out which moves the entire volume of gas around the machine. This ensures that the air in the machine passes through the scrubber where carbon dioxide is removed and then oxygen added. On open circuit every breath you take is carbon dioxide free, so the effect of breathing fast and shallow is that you are not removing carbon dioxide and so are accumulating carbon dioxide in your body. On a machine you are re-breathing the same breath, so if you are breathing fast and shallow the machine does not have time to get rid of the carbon dioxide, which means that every new breath has more and more carbon dioxide in it. The gas in the machine is literally becoming more and more toxic with each breath.

Dave understood the problems of exertion at depth and as he struggled with Deon, he noticed that he had started to breathe heavily. He instantly stopped, recognising that staying could kill him, and started his ascent. I doubt if there was any question in his own mind as to whether or not he would dive again to retrieve Deon. The only question was when.

We slowly packed up and made our way back to warm showers and hot food, idly chatting about the challenge that lay ahead – retrieving Deon. I had gone from no longer wanting to dive deep (I had the record I wanted and more importantly proven to myself that it was not a fluke, I could control my mind and fear) but now with Deon lying within reach my interest had been piqued. This was a challenge a different challenge. Going deeper would be more of the same thing, a quick bounce and proving that your mind can control your body but to retrieve Deon a diver had to re-write standard diving practice. This was a dive no one had done before and the challenge fascinated me. How would you solve the problems of exertion at depth, never mind how would you (with minimum effort) get Deon from the mud to the surface?

I was not alone in my ponderings and that night at supper (to all of our surprise) Dave asked us if we could stay on until Sunday. He wanted to go back and finish what he had started. It was Thursday and I had never seen a deep diver seriously consider doing what amounted to two world record dives in a period of four days. No matter how fit you are, a deep dive that lasts over eight hours takes its toll on your body. Even Nuno (who is supremely fit) gives his body six months to a year to recover and here Dave was planning to go back in a matter of days. It made sense from a logistics perspective as the site was already set up. Diving so quickly would also mean that by the time the media found out it would be all over so we would avoid the drama and sensationalism that we instinctively knew would come hand in hand with this discovery. Was diving so quickly a safe decision?

I wasn't familiar with the constraints, or in this case, freedoms that a machine created. On top of which, the only person who can ever know if a dive is safe is the diver himself. Both Dave and Don were exuding confidence so who was I to challenge their reality? They would go ahead with or without our help. We were tempted, but, it had been a long two weeks and we all wanted to be back home. An extra four days did not sound like much fun, even if we would be part of history in the making.

The decision was made for us on Friday morning at breakfast when Dave asked us if we were still planning on leaving and if so, could we give him a lift to the chamber. Turns out his body had felt the effects of a dive so deep and his elbow had bent during the night. To quote Dave, that put paid to a second attempt on Sunday. We packed and dropped him off at the chamber on the way home.

Preparing to Change Reality

A chamber is a lonely place with a lot of time to sit and think and that is exactly what Dave did - think about how and when he was going to go back to fetch Deon. In the meantime, the news that Deon had been found spread through the diving community and as expected, found its way into the mainstream. Finding and retrieving Deon became news headlines. The fact that two world records had been set on the same trip was completely lost. It would take another four months for the Guinness Book of World records to recognise my record and by then deep cave diving would be notorious, as would the name Dave Shaw.

Derek and Gordon (the cameraman from my dive) had immediately become involved in the planning of the recovery attempt. If successful, it would be a world first and put not only re-breathers, but Don and Dave squarely on the map. It would also make a brilliant documentary. From them I heard that the dive was scheduled for early January and was restricted to re-breather divers, which meant not only was I not invited, but pretty much every other technical diver in the country was as well. The choice to use only re-breather divers was only one of a number of controversial decisions on this dive and it was a deliberate choice, made to showcase the power, versatility and safety of re-breathers. Not that they were short of divers; everyone wanted to be on this dive.

Sitting outside the dive, the rest of the diving community thought they were mad. Why go and fetch Deon personally? Why not send a remote vehicle? Whilst I understood how irresistible this challenge was, I was finding it hard to put the allure into words. How do you explain the attraction of a problem that had never been solved before? Recovering a body from 272 meters would take all of Dave and Don's experience not to mention talent and creative thinking to find the right solution and get it right.

It was difficult to be on the outside of this dive, even if I did understand. Part of me wanted to be involved, another wasn't so sure. When something goes wrong on a deep dive (especially one that was receiving so much press as this one), it damages the reputations of everyone involved. The world assigns responsibility to everyone, even though the reality is that the only people who would be making the decisions would be Dave and Don. Did I want to be connected to a dive that stood a good chance of failing spectacularly?

It turned out to be a moot point. Two weeks before the scheduled date I was asked if I would be surface marshall. I wrestled with the decision. Did I not get involved and so retain some distance should things go wrong? The only problem with that was that if something did go wrong I had no ability to make a difference. Besides, I had been there at the beginning of the story and I wanted to be part of the end of it. I put my doubts aside and said yes.

I wasn't close to the planning of the dive and there was no real time to interrogate either Dave or Don to get details. Christmas was upon us and my focus was on family, not diving. Behind the scenes Don and Dave were putting the final touches to their plans; Anne (Dave's wife) was sewing the body bag out of silk, Gordon was furiously getting a head cam made that could withstand the depth and the rest of us were enjoying our Christmases and New Years. The dive was planned for Saturday the 8th January and like most of the team, I arrived the Tuesday before. It was the 4th of January and I did not recognise Boesmansgat. The place was packed. The dive site had been taken over by police divers with a huge portable chamber taking up what little flat space there was at the top. The lodge where we stayed was overflowing with divers and families. The only familiar faces were that of Derek and Gordon. This was most definitely not a quiet family affair.

The first night we were all introduced to one another and I was handed the dive plan. I was furiously taking notes trying to learn the names of the divers I had to manage, while listening to the outline of the plan. The prime concern was to get Deon to the surface as quickly as possible. Legally we had to pass Deon to police divers who would take control of his body and move him to the closest morgue where they would commence a thorough investigation into his death before handing him back to his parents.

Dave was planning to place Deon in a body bag to prevent loss of any skeletal remains on ascent. He would then pass Deon to Don at 220 meters. Dusan and Mark Andrews would be waiting at 150 meters where they would check that Don was OK. Don would proceed to 100 meters and pass Deon to Pieter Herbst, who would then take Deon to the police divers who would be waiting at 20 meters Deon should surface in 70 minutes. Don and Dave would take eight and twelve hours respectively.

Three other divers would check up on Dave and Don, Lo Vingerling at 100 meters, Steven Sanders at 80 meters and then finally, Gerhard Du Preez and Truwan Laas who would be doing 50m and shallower support for the rest of the day.

Following their usual strategy, there was no intention to have continuous support at any point in the dive. Shallow support divers would pop in and check on both Don and Dave every hour. Other than that, they were content to be on their own. If something went wrong they felt they would be able to solve it and didn't need anyone else's help.

Medical support was also a priority, with Dr Jack Meintjies joining the team to support Malcolm Smith, our friendly paramedic. Dr Jack would be responsible for making any medical decisions and implementing a recompression treatment in the chamber and Malcolm (who had been on my trip) would be responsible for getting an injured diver from the hole up to the doc.

The mood was buoyant and optimistic as we started the first day's diving, tackling the veritable mountain of cylinders that had to be staged at the right depths on the shot line. Over twenty cylinders had to get the right dvs and then be put on the right place on the shot line. This was the gas that could mean the difference between life and death not only for Don and Dave, but for anyone of the eight support divers who would be in and out for the duration of the dive.

The hole (which is always short of space), was overpopulated with every flat surface and every rock holding a person or piece of kit. Even the cliff wall was busy, with a team of riggers preparing a pulley that they intended to use to get Dave into the chamber as quickly as possible if anything went wrong. To all appearances, Dave and Don had thought this one through thoroughly.

I was fascinated. If successful, this dive would redefine what was possible with scuba diving, making open circuit redundant. Dave Shaw was the first person to take a machine successfully deeper than 200 meters. This time round Don would be matching my own record depth of 220 meters and in order to get around the design constraints of his machine had had to do some extensive customisation of his own. No out of the box machine is rated for diving to depths below 150 meters, however, by replacing the standard electronics with a Hammerhead *and* then flooding that with liquid paraffin to remove *all* airspaces you are able to take a standard machine to well, we don't know yet what the limits are - Dave set it at 272 meters.

Every night we sat down and went over the plan for the next day. It was in these meetings that Dave and Don emphasised the fact that if something was to go wrong, no one was to risk their own lives. Dave even went so far as to request that if he did die with Deon, no one was to go and retrieve him. The other statement that was repeatedly made was that if anything went wrong, I would be the only person allowed to make decisions in my capacity as surface marshall. Everyone else (including the police divers) would be expected to follow my instructions. I suddenly started to feel woefully unprepared. I knew how to be Don and Dave underwater facing the challenges of staying alive but I had never had to make decisions on the surface that could affect other people's lives.

I was desperately hoping that my job would be nothing more than telling people when they had to get into the water followed by the long tedium of waiting for Dave and Don to surface. The only problem was, what if that wasn't how it went down? If it went wrong I wouldn't have the luxury of time to make decisions. Nor would I have the ability to abdicate responsibility. So I started to visualise what my options were, going through different scenarios and options. I wanted to be prepared.

Don and Dave were focusing on their dives and without any directions to the contrary, I tried to organise the support dives, checking to see if we would have any congestion problems. With so many divers in the water I expected that the plans would mean that divers would be fighting for space at six meters. It wasn't easy. No one was using set paper dive plans. They were all using computers that dynamically generated their decompression schedules so no one could tell me where they would be at any point in time. I did my best and generated a schedule that would give all the support divers first a twenty minute and then a ten minute warning to ensure that they were ready on time. Two days before the actual dive we did a dry run to iron out any glitches in the plan. It was all going well.

Diving wasn't the only thing we were focusing on. True to form I came down with the dreaded Boesmansgat lurgy, although this time I managed to avoid the nausea and only suffered from diarrhea. It was the day of the mock dive and I wasn't the only one suffering. One by one the whole dive team came down with various versions and we quickly ran out of medicine to get tummies under control. No one was prepared to miss the mock up, so we all made do. To make matters worse it was January in the Karoo, which meant that it was beyond hot! The rooms were stifling and sleep was hard to get because of the heat.

With the mock up dive out of the way all that was left to do was take a day to relax and then dive. Not that it was really a day off - preparations were still being made. Dave's helmet cam was fitted, team photos taken and press conferences held until all that remained left on the 'to do' list was the dive itself. We were as ready as we could be. As we did our final brief Dave and Don reiterated that if something were to go wrong, the support divers were to look after themselves. No heroics.

It was a stance that the outside world didn't understand. For people who didn't dive, the fact that Dave had made plans to manage his death was interpreted as foreboding, some even saying that he was actively courting death. In the real world you don't analyse and prepare for all the consequences of your actions - and you definitely don't talk about or acknowledge the bad ones. In the real world that's interpreted as actively asking for something bad to happen. Yet in my world the ability to understand all the consequences of a dive, including your own death, is critical if you want to stand any chance of surviving. We plan for the worst which I believe is the only responsible thing to do. It is one thing to place your own life on the line (relying on your family and friends to manage their pain should you die), it is quite another to do so without saying goodbyes or making sure your life was in order.

The Day We Never Expected

Dave liked to dive early so at four am alarm clocks rang and we started our day. Today it was even more important that we have some daylight at the end of the dive to manage unexpected situations.

It was cold and dark at the hole. It was also quiet. I never did get to say good luck and goodbye. Shortly after six am Dave started his dive and I started my stopwatch. So far so good. I would only relax when the police divers returned with Deon. That would mean Dave and Don were on their way up, and from there we should be able to manage most things.

13 minutes after Dave started his dive, Don started his. The strain was showing on the faces of Theo and Marie Dryer

(Deon's parents). It seemed useless to tell them that at that moment Dave would be placing their son in the bag and starting his ascent, yet it felt right to try and verbalise what was happening underwater.

23 minutes came. "If all is going well, Dave has just handed Deon to Don at 220 meters." My words cut through the still morning air.

Six minutes later and I mentally checked off Dusan and Mark at 150 meters (the first and deepest of the support divers). Time was passing slowly and when Pieter started his dive 47 minutes in I was relieved. This meant that Deon was well on his way back to his parents. Seven minutes after that, Lo started his dive to check on Don at 105 meters.

We now had six divers in the water. Behind me, the police divers started to get ready for their part. All around people waited. Finally, it was time for the police team to get in and fetch Deon at 20 meters. Only 60 minutes had passed since we had said goodbye to Dave.

10 minutes passed (70 minutes runtime). By this point Deon would be with the police divers and on the final leg of his journey. The last two support divers, Truwan and Gerhard were starting to get kitted up, which marked the start of what was to be the longest portion of the day, waiting for Don and Dave to get out.

It should have taken the police divers minutes to bring Deon from 20 meters to the surface. Instead, minutes passed and there was no sign of anyone in the water. The observers started to get restless. The silence was absolute.

We waited.

Finally, twenty minutes after they left and ten minutes late, the police divers surfaced empty handed. They had not seen a single diver. I double checked. "You are sure there are no divers in sight below you? No lights?" The answer was no - which was wrong. There should have been divers within sight. Something had not gone according to plan.

You could feel the stillness in the air as the doubts started to creep into people's minds. I wasn't overly concerned. The dive plan had been fluid, allowing Dave different options to manage whatever he found. Whilst he had planned for a five minute bottom, Dave had also taken plans for anything up to seven minutes. The best case scenario was that it had taken him longer than expected which meant that the whole plan would be delayed. I wasn't prepared to entertain the worst case scenario.

We waited.

Dave's plan had been to slip Deon into a silk bag. If Deon was too difficult to move, Dave would attempt to recover just his head. Either way, he would be closely monitoring his time. For every 30 seconds extra, he would have to do an extra half hour of decompression and he was already on the limits of his machine. I was trying not to worry about any of the other divers. They were all on machines so had time if something went wrong. They all had dive computers so they could stay longer and still know how much decompression to do.

The second round of police divers got into the water and went to wait back to 20 meters to wait.

I was watching the surface of the water impatiently and was finally rewarded with a diver, Derek I believe. He had taken the camera down with the police divers and I could see from his face it wasn't good news. It was 90 minutes after Dave had left. In Derek's hand was a slate. It said simply:

"Waited at 150m for six minutes. Lights below us! Dave, Don?"

Both Derek and I read that slate and both Derek and I interpreted it as telling us that there were no divers below Dusan and Mark (150 meters). I was stunned. At the back of my mind I had accepted that Dave might not be coming back, but I had never imagined that Don wouldn't. My day of boredom had just drastically changed. It was seven thirty in the morning and against all expectation we were now looking at our worst-case scenario – both of our deep divers were lost, probably dead.

Perched on the rocks behind me the police divers watched and waited for instructions from me. All around me, people reacted. Derek in particular reacted with action, forgetting the instructions that the surface marshall was the one in charge should something go wrong. He started instructing the remaining two support divers. As I stood there the dive became a rope that was suddenly starting to come apart, each strand unwrapping as I lost control of the dive. Clear in my head were Don's words the night before: "The only person who has the power to make decisions on the surface is Verna. Only if she gives away control may anyone else take over."

I simply didn't have the luxury of feeling sorry for myself or complaining. I had to get control of what was happening. Only thing was, I had no idea what to do. Everyone was expecting me to do something, but if we had lost both divers there was simply nothing to do.

And then more news. The one change we had made based on the dry run was to rig a bell on the shotline and set a separate line onto which divers could clip a slate allowing us to get information out of the water faster. Derek rushed over and grabbed the slate as it was pulled out of the water. His voice was strained as he read out the news - Dave wasn't coming back, Don was OK.

I breathed a sigh of relief and then realised I had just accepted the death of a man I had greatly admired without a second thought. There was no time to deal with the emotional impact of that slate. We had lost Dave and that would all have to wait until we had Don and every other diver safely out of the water.

I had no idea what had gone wrong but I did know that Don would have gone to help Dave, which meant he was ascending from a dive that was way deeper than he had planned. In fact, everyone would have overstayed, pushing their own bottom times and their depths waiting for Dave and Don to return so that they could assist. The radio was crackling as the doctor passed on his own set of instructions. It seemed the common consensus was that I had to send one of the two remaining support divers to 100 meters to look for Dave.

I was being pushed for a decision and I still had no idea what to do. With all the commotion and disbelief around me I couldn't think. I had no time to think. I also had no time to get it wrong. I walked away, taking Dave's dive plans with me. I started to think like a diver. Dave was supposed to have reached 272 meters 15 minutes after he left the surface. That meant by the time Don got to 220 meters Dave would have been diving for over 23 minutes, and at the bottom for almost ten minutes – three minutes longer than his most extreme worst case plan. I tried to place myself in Dave's place and couldn't avoid the truth of the situation - if he had not been able to solve the problem and get himself onto the main shotline and ascending in ten minutes he was dead and there wasn't a thing anyone else could do.

I looked around me and realised that my job was as much managing the people who were watching as the divers. Even though Dave had time on his machine and whilst it was unrealistic to think that he could spend more than 20 minutes at 272 meters and come back alive, his machine did give him that option. I couldn't deny him that option or deny the observers the luxury of hope. If I were Dave, the last thing I would want would be for the people on the surface to give up on me. I would hope that my support divers would leave me a beacon - something that would help me find my way back.

I revised my plan and walked back into the chaos. The first thing I had to do was take back control of the dive. To that end I walked over to Derek as he was instructing Gerhard and politely asked him to stop making my decisions. I then asked Gerhard to get into the water and find out who was where and more importantly, if everyone was all right. I also asked him to take a flashlight and attach it at the ceiling so that if Dave did find his way back he would at least have a reference point. He wasn't allowed to go deeper than 50 meters, unless there was a situation he needed to manage and he was asked for assistance. He was one of only two divers who had not been deep and so could get in and out of the water without decompressing and I needed to keep it that way. Besides, I had this feeling that Don's idea of having two divers who spent ten minutes in the water every hour was going to be completely insufficient. I wanted to be able to provide continuous support if needed.

Once again I waited. There were no other decisions to be made. Truwan was kitted up and ready to go. I had the police divers on standby as well as Derek. Now I needed to find out if Don was still on his machine. If he was on open circuit I would have to closely monitor the gas on the line to ensure he had enough for his whole dive. I was furiously trying to work out how I was going to manage the next six hours with only two support divers and hoping that no one had pushed their limits too far. I was desperately hoping that we didn't have a bent diver on our hands. We only had one chamber, it could only take one diver … and everyone had broken their dive plans.

I was also getting frustrated not being in the water. I had no idea what was going on. It was very tempting to just grab my own kit and go and find out for myself, but that would have meant there would be no one on the surface with diving experience to make decisions. I stayed put and yes, waited.

It seemed to take forever for Gerhard to come back with news, but at least it was good news. Don seemed to be fine. His one dive computer had blown as had his hammerhead which meant he had no electronics and was running his machine manually. His remaining dive computer showed he had reached a depth of 227 meters which was shallower than I was expecting and a relief. With Gerhard also came a very clear message that Dave wasn't coming back.

It was obvious that Don had started to go to Dave's assistance and then had to turn around when his machine imploded. I was impressed that he was able to recover the situation at that depth and worried that as a result he would have to go onto open circuit which would have added hours to his already eight hour dive plan and exposed him to the added risk of hypothermia. I still didn't trust that nothing would go wrong between 60 meters and 30 meters (both notorious points for deep water bends) but the day seemed salvageable. I started to work out how to give Don 100% coverage from 50 meters and up. At least no one else was in trouble and everyone seemed to be in control of their dives.

Truwan was next into the water, having waited for Gerhard to report back so that I could give him revised instructions. His task was simple: go and stay with Don for twenty minutes and then come back. We started to relax and settle in for the day. I was expecting to alternate Truwan and Gerhard on twenty minute dives until Steve, Lo and Pieter were out and had recovered enough to start diving again. Then they could get in and give Gerhard and Truwan a welcome rest. But Truwan didn't came back. I finally sent Gerhard in to find out what on earth had happened. We were four and a half hours into the dive.

Truwan finally re-appeared and the news he brought pretty much shattered any semblance of control and calm we might have recovered. He had found Don at 50 meters but, Don was vomiting violently, completely disorientated and barely able to function. I was stunned. There had been a space of maybe five, at most ten minutes between when Gerhard left Don and Truwan had arrived. The knowledge that in that short time period we could have lost Don was simply beyond belief. Thank heavens I had no time to obsess over it.

We were now in a totally different scenario. One minute I had enough divers to manage support, now I had a seriously ill diver at 50 meters and all my divers had decompression obligation. Don was critically ill and wouldn't be able to get himself to the surface unaided. Common consensus was that he had suffered from a counter diffusion bend in his inner ear, which normally results in a complete loss of balance. Divers would have to be with him all the time, never leaving him alone for even a minute. To make it worse, he was on open circuit, which meant that this was no longer an 8 hour dive, but a 12 hour one. He was also too deep. To keep someone with him full time until he got to 20 meters would mean that each diver was clocking up decompression of his own. Derek (as the only cave-trained diver on site) was upgraded to support. On open circuit he could only stay with Don for minutes, but it would give Truwan and Gerhard some extra time - enough I hoped for one of the other support divers to get out, spend two hours recovering on the surface and then get back in again.

Over the next three hours first Gerhard, Truwan and then Steve followed finally by Lo all cycled 30 minute stays with Don, with Derek on open circuit doing ten to 15 minutes stints to give the guys a break. Pieter came out the water with a sore knee so was relegated to helping Doc get the chamber ready for Don. Which left Malcolm (the paramedic), Doctor Jack (Meintjies) and myself trying to predict what was happening and what needed to be done next.

Not that we had much time for forward planning for those first two hours. We were fire fighting, trying to get gas for Derek's cylinders, extra cylinders for the decompressing support divers and finding dvs. It was one thing after another. Dael (Dusan's wife) stepped in and picked up one of the balls I simply could not manage, monitoring who was in, who was out and how long everyone had been spending - which meant that I could at least keep track of how much decompression the support divers were racking up and make plans to keep them out of the water for as long as possible.

Our first challenge was ensuring that Don didn't disappear on us, and to that end we literally tied him to the shot line. Something that didn't make him very happy. Whilst he was still coherent, the support divers had to do a large portion of his diving for him, making sure he was switching gases and ascending as his dive computer required. He was on open circuit, which was a real concern because it meant he would be losing heat fast. He was also dehydrating badly thanks to the combination of vomiting and being on open circuit. It wasn't looking good. On the up side, even though every time the divers got out of the water they reported that Don was in a bad way, they also said he still was functioning and thinking.

I turned around and asked Malcolm if there was anything we could give Don underwater to stop the vomiting. Gerhard was also a paramedic and between the two of them they create a concoction in a syringe to take to Don. We weren't overly optimistic that it would work, but we had to try. The idea was that the syringe would enable Don to get all of the meds into his mouth and not lose it to the surrounding water. Don managed to get most of the medicine in and then promptly threw it up. We tried a different strategy, just sending down energy drinks and water to try and replace some of what he was losing.

Whilst we were doing everything we could, we all knew that the only chance Don had was staying in the water and the only way that would happen was if he stayed conscious. I wanted it to be very clear in everyone's minds exactly what was expected of them underwater. I didn't want Don dying there and someone blaming themselves. Between Dr Jack and Malcolm we gave the entire support team explicit instructions. We were to keep Don in the water for as long as we could. If he lost consciousness and was still breathing, he stayed in the water. If he stopped breathing then he was to be brought to the surface as fast as possible.

There is a simplicity to these situations that is quite blunt in its application: so long as Don was breathing he was alive, and we were committed to doing whatever we had to in order to keep him that way. When it came to decision-making we chose the option that gave us hope. In this case, even though bringing Don out would in all probability kill him, if he wasn't breathing underwater he was definitely dead. Probably dead was better than definitely dead.

My aim in the first hours was just to keep Don in the water doing his decompression and finding a way for the rest of us to manage the stress of the day, so out came the paramedic rules. After all, it did seem appropriate.

Rule 1:

If you drop the baby, pick it up.

Rule 2:

All bleeding eventually stops.

Rule 3:

Sooner or later, all patients die.

Somehow they broke the tension and allowed us to laugh again. With some effort we instilled a sense of normality into the day and as the hours passed I started to think we might actually pull this off. Never did I think that Don would manage to stay down for his entire decompression (almost 12 hours). I really expected that we would be forced to bring him to the surface early.

The afternoon wore on and we settled into a rhythm at the water's edge. At the top of the hole the chamber was being prepared and I started to wonder what was going on back home. Had the news broken? It had been Derek's responsibility to pass the news on to Hong Kong and Dave's wife and we were waiting his return. The news he brought back was perturbing, someone had leaked the story to the press and the lodge was swarming with reporters trying to get details. I was suddenly intensely happy that there were armed soldiers at the gate to the hole. Having reporters on site would have made the day unbearable.

As the day turned to night, Don finally reached the last leg of his dive, six meters. To our relief, as he had come up his condition had improved to the point where he was able to interact with the divers around him. He was still having co-ordination problems but at least he was able to chat. With his arrival at six meters came the order from Doc that he was to get out. Not news that Don was particularly happy about. He still had three hours of decompression to go and he knew as well as I did that breaking decompression was a sure fire way of bending. I knew I had a fight on my hands to get Don to break his decompression, but the Doc was adamant. Don either got out when told to or the Doc was going home and Don was on his own. We sent a slate back down telling Don he would be getting out, by force if required. He agreed.

Twelve hours and 34 minutes after Dave started his dive, Don surfaced. It took the team 22 minutes to get him from the water to the chamber 150 meters above us. An unprecedented feat for Boesmansgat.

My job finished when the stretcher started to lift Don away from us. I officially handed Don over to Pieter and the Doc, and started to pack up. The sun was already setting and at the water's edge it was starting to get chilly. After all the buzz and mayhem, it was suddenly quiet. The action had moved away from us, following Don. I was glad that it was over, glad that my part was done and that it was now someone else's responsibility. After all the good humour and conversation of the day we all went strangely quiet. We each gathered our belongings and started to climb out.

I felt drained and numb. I needed to talk about what happened, to process it and find out how I felt about it. I wanted to get back, have a shower and some food. I had already asked Derek to make sure there were no reporters back at the lodge; the last thing we needed was for a reporter to take our discussions out of context. I was also worried that people I had at home had heard what had happened and were worrying about me.

As I reached the top I grabbed my phone and started telling family and friends that I was OK but that Dave wasn't coming back. We still had no clear idea of what had happened. Each support diver had a piece of the puzzle and no one had had the time to hear each story yet.

Putting it All Together

The full story had to wait until after dinner and it was with some effort that we all collected late in the evening to relate the sequence of events as it happened. Dusan and Mark were the first to start the tale. They had reached 150 meters and waited five minutes longer than their planned time with absolutely nothing below them. Just as they were about to leave they said they saw a single light coming up. They had no idea who it was. That was the first slate we received. "One Light Below, Don or Dave" Their handwriting had been so bad we had read the 'one' as a 'no' – "No lights below, Don or Dave?" They had ended up doing a punishing five hour dive instead of their expected three hours.

Then came Pieter, who told us how, realising that things had gone wrong, he had gone from his planned 100 meters to 120 meters to find out who was coming up. He was rewarded with the sight of Don but couldn't stay long enough to actually meet up with him. Next was Lo who was supposed to wait at 100 meters but seeing Don below him he had made the decision to go down and assist. He found Don at 118 meters, something he failed to tell me when he told me that he was able to get back into the water after only two hours on the surface (I would have made him wait another hour before putting him back in the water if I had known his real depth). Lo was the one who first found out what had happened.

Steve was next as he reached his target depth of 80 meters he had met Lo who handed over Don's slate. On reading what was written he had turned and rushed to the surface, cutting his decompression to the bare minimum to get the news back to us as fast as possible. This was the second slate telling us that Dave wasn't coming back but that Don was OK.

There was only one piece of the puzzle missing, Don's. We were hoping he could tell us something about Dave. Sunday dawned bright and sunny and it was hard to believe that Saturday had in fact happened. Don arrived from a night in the chamber looking awful - alive, but awful. He couldn't walk and barely had the energy to keep his eyes open. I can still see him propped up on the bed, one eye half open telling us what had happened.

From 150 meters he had been able see Dave's light far below him but there had been no bubbles or movement, which there should have been because Dave should have already been coming back up. Don had decided to continue past his meeting point down to Dave. Even though his one remaining dive computer read 227 meters, his impression was that he reached the 250 meter mark when his electronics imploded. At that depth he should have had the bottom squarely in sight, but had no recollection of it. With his electronics imploded, there was nothing for it but to turn around and focus on getting himself out of the water.

In Don's words: "After the implosion I still had one set of electronics that monitored but didn't control the re-breather. I went to my open circuit cylinders while I stabilised the re-breather — an 11 litre cylinder only lasting three minutes at that depth. Then I went back to the re-breather and drove it manually. This was fine - a much-practiced technique. In my mind I was still hoping that Dave would follow ... The ascent carried on as normal, I left extra cylinders in the water, just in case. Peter Herbst was the first diver I met at 124m, by this time I was sure that Dave wasn't following."

As for what happened at 50 meters? Don's description was chilling. One moment he was fine, the next the world started spinning. He saw the shotline moving away from him and instinctively grabbed it. If he hadn't, he would have simply sunk to the bottom and joined Deon and Dave.

The Video We Never Expected to See

We still had no idea what had happened to Dave, and like most of the team I needed to be back at work the next day so I packed up and went home, leaving Pieter and the police divers to pull out the shotline and all the kit.

What happened next stunned and surprised all of us - Dave and Deon came up with the line. After all that, Dave had fulfilled his promise and returned Deon to the light of day and his parents. More importantly for us, we would find out what had happened at the bottom that day. His helmet camera was still there, with every minute of the dive waiting ...

I had to force myself to watch that underwater footage. Even today it sends shivers down my spine and brings tears to my eyes. We watched as Dave descended, the line in his hand. Even on film the silence is eerie, with no bubbles to mark his passage. As he reached the bottom of the shotline it became obvious that he was breathing too fast. I felt myself screaming at him to stop and breathe. But he carried on ... oblivious. I had to remind myself that this had already happened, and we were nothing more than privileged witnesses.

As Dave arrived at Deon 12 minutes into his dive (well within his dive time) we saw what he saw, Deon was floating in the water and not stuck in the mud. This was not what Dave had planned for. Perhaps he should have turned around at that point, after all this was a scenario he had not planned, but with all the effort that goes into one of these dives I doubt I would have made the decision to abort the dive. Besides, whether he turned immediately or whether he stayed his full bottom time, he still had the same amount of decompression ahead of him. He had five minutes to try recover Deon – nothing ventured, nothing gained.

The video counted out the last minutes of Dave's life relentlessly. With the body floating he was struggling. He put his hand held torch down on the mud to free his hands and still illuminate the site. It not only showed Deon, but also a mess of fine white line. As a cave divers our reaction was predictable, what was all that line doing in such a mess around him? It was dangerous, it could trap him. He seemed to be still in control though, monitoring his time every 30 seconds until he reached his planned five minutes at which point he stopped what he was doing and started to retreat.

By this time his breathing was way out of control. I watched in disbelief as he tried to get back to the main line but found he was stuck. Keen observation of the tape indicated that it was his light head that had been tangled in a loop in the line. He tried to find the problem and started to get his scissors to cut himself free. And then it all went still. I didn't need to see more. I got up and left. Outside I found the dive team scattered around the garden, trying to reign in the tears and make sense of what we had just seen.

Can any of us ever know what his last moments were like? Probably not, but I found myself wondering if my experiences trapped in the incline shaft were similar to Dave's. I had been where he had been. I had almost not made it back. I knew that could have happened to me. And, I knew that he had known that he was in trouble and he might not make it out, just like I had. The only comforting thought for me was the fact that I knew he would have been calm. Just as I had been at 152 meters, there would have been no fear and no pain. He just went to sleep. He had run out of time. Maybe, maybe if he had made it back to the line or bailed out onto the open circuit he carried he would have bought himself precious time. Maybe he could have made it back out then.

He hadn't.

The Truth, is Relative

As the world moved on, the story of Dave and Deon passed out of the public's eye. We were still waiting for the final report to find out if there was something, anything, that he could have done to change the outcome of that day. Not that it mattered to him, but it seemed important to understand why he paid the highest of prices. As a community we also wanted to make sure that no one else died making the same mistakes. One life, was enough.

What killed him? The official report states carbon dioxide build up which increased his narcosis to over 70 meters. This would have meant he was battling to think coherently, never mind retain control of his actions. Was there a single thing he could have done that would have made a difference? I believe that if he managed to gain control of his breathing right at the beginning he would have stood a chance. Then, when he found himself caught in the line he would have been able to think faster, with more clarity and possibly get himself untangled. He never should have become entangled in his line at all, that was the second mistake: placing his hand held torch on the ground where it could hook the line. You never leave your light head on the ground where it can get entangled, never.

The list of things Dave could have done and did not do is long. If he had bailed onto open circuit he might have been able to recover from the carbon dioxide poisoning. If he had used a helmet to attach his torch and so keep his hands free he would not have had to place the torch head on the ground, or if he had stowed his light properly then he would not have found himself trapped. If he had made the decision to turn when arriving to find that the situation wasn't the one he had planned for … if, if, if. It wasn't one thing that killed him. It never is.

His actions or lack of them made no difference to the outcome of this dive, and no matter how outspoken the armchair divers in the world are, I will firmly and strongly fight for Dave's right to decide. It was his life, he was the only one who had the right to decide if that dive was worth it or if he was ready for it.

But was it the right decision? As we started to talk about the dive, trying to find that one 'silver' bullet that we could blame, some worrying facts started to come to light and I started to wonder if Dave really had been ready. One of the cylinders that Dave should have bailed onto would have killed him - it was a 40 meter mix and not a 270 meter mix. So even if Dave had made bailed out to manage his carbon dioxide and made it back to the line he still would have died. This is a rookie mistake to make for a man who was trying to be the world's deepest and best diver. Yet, was it his? He had not been the one filling his cylinders, he had given that responsibility to his right hand man, Don. But, he should have checked and double checked every cylinder regardless of who was filling them and marked them himself. I do! No way am I going to trust my life to anyone else. If I die, it must be all my fault.

Even more shocking was that fact that there was a very good reason why Don's electronics imploded, which was the directly contributing cause to his almost lethal bend at 50 meters. He and Dave had spent most of the night before the dive trying to repair a problem with the battery. Not only had they both had insufficient sleep, but Don had (against all advice, including that of the manufacturer of his controller) decided to dive on compromised equipment. He had got the electronics back up and running but he had not had enough liquid paraffin to re-fill the controls, which left a visible air bubble that he knew meant that there was a very, very good chance it would implode at depth. His support divers had challenged him and his comment to them shocked me even further. He turned around and bluntly told them "I have come too far and done too much to turn around now".

I was stunned! This was the man who had spent hours convincing me that he wasn't like other deep divers (the Nuno's of the world if you like), ego bound and chasing after glory, and yet his own words seemed to totally deny that fact. There are simply times on a dive, no matter how far you have come, no matter how confident you are in your own abilities, when you simply have to walk away. It is one of Nuno's greatest strengths – he knows when to walk away.

That one statement has made me doubt everything I thought I knew about both Dave and Don. Did Dave and Don succumb to summit fever? Of all the deep divers I have met, Dave was one of the least ego-driven. Yet, he stood there that night and didn't turn the dive when perhaps he should have. Was there one thing that could have saved Dave's life? I think that maybe there was – Don!

Dave and Don were an impressive team. Dave had an ambition and drive that lit something inside of Don. Until then, Don had never been interested in deep exploration. He had spent six years at Badgat and never gone into the incline shaft, never explored beyond what had already been done. I have begun to suspect that Dave's success was in part founded on Don's extensive experience. To get where he did, so fast, with so little time in the water makes sense when you have a Don in the background. Dave trusted Don implicitly and that is where I start to get uncomfortable. It is almost like they were not two independent divers, but one diver. As if Dave handed over a part of the decision-making (and responsibility), never questioning Don. Don's glory was based on Dave's willingness to place his life on the line.

More importantly, I can't help but wonder if Don had decided to call that dive, whether Dave would have stopped and listened. I can't help but think he would have. Dave trusted Don, implicitly. When I dive, I have Joseph. He is the one who can keep a clear head and not get blinded by dive fever. He is the one I listen to when he tells me to call a dive, and I listen because I know he wants me alive more than he wants me to be successful. On Dave's dive he had Don, who had come too far and done to much to turn back. He wanted the dive more than Dave did.

Being an explorer is not about gambling with your life. It is about making choices. You have to be able to be honest enough with yourself to realise when you are no longer making sane decisions. You have to know when it is no longer about the dive but about the glory.

(6) Ego, Control, Power; the Magic Cocktail

Records are fleeting things. The fact that I had set a new world record for depth for women barely made local headlines, never mind national or international ones. Perhaps it inspired one or two women who were passionate about diving, but it hardly created more than a ripple in the world. It took Dave's death to do that.

Why do we risk our lives for a label? What drove Dave to want to be deepest? The list of people who have gotten it wrong and died for glory is long … and growing. Why do those of us who choose this want it soo much?

Looking back over my journey and the divers I have met, Nuno, Dave, Don (to name a few), it is hard to find a single or even easy answer. Is it the glory? Because I can see no glory in Dave's death, only consequences that were, in the end, not even paid by him, coupled with a nagging feeling that we did not live up to our responsibility. If we had walked away from the dive, all of us, would he still have gotten into the water?

Is it about being deepest and so standing apart from the rest of the world? Pedestals are hard to resist: we spend most of our lives looking up to people, thinking how much better life must be from on top of that pedestal. It is easy to think that by following in Dave's footsteps (or mine) you too could have an easy and successful life.

But what is glory and pursuit of labels other than your ego shouting to be seen and heard? We all want recognition and no matter who you are, there will always be ego involved in deep diving, always! Not one of us, not Dave, not Don, not Nuno, not even I can claim to not have been driven in some part by our egos. We try and find more noble reasons, instinctively knowing that the world will not be attracted by such an ugly and selfish thing as ego, but it is always there - sometimes strong, sometimes weak, but always there.

Part of what got me to 186 meters was a need for recognition, but it was not the whole reason. This fatal flaw I seem to have acquired is a complex beast, hard to pin down. Yes, I wanted recognition, but not that of the world's. I wanted it from the people who had so easily dismissed me – Nuno for one and way back in my past, my dad ...

I wanted the label 'deepest' more than I wanted to live because getting it was supposed to turn me into someone else and I desperately needed to be someone else, someone who was in control and had the power to manage her own destiny. Someone who was no longer afraid and who was happy. I had started out needing only to be part of a team, but then as the people around me rejected me, it became bigger. It became something I needed to prove to the world. I needed the world to believe I was special and good enough ... so that I could.

Was it my ego I was struggling with, or was it my past? I no longer need external recognition to create peace in my mind, these days my ego has to work harder to throw me off balance. Now it is about holding on. It is hard to sit back and be comfortable as other women set their sights on taking away *my* record. And it is my record, bought with my tears. I was the first to challenge the world of men and I was the one who paid the price. This is mine and my ego does not want to share it. I never know whether to laugh or cry when these moods hit me because my real self knows that records are meant to be broken.

Most days I am content with the fact that one day I will no longer be the deepest woman in the world - that label will belong to someone else and her struggle will have been every bit as hard as mine. But some days, some days it is hard to remember what this is really all about and I have to work hard to resist the temptation of going deeper and deeper - making it harder for the women to catch up and harder for the men to ignore me. Those are the days I stay away from the water because I know that the dive that kills me will be the one I do because my ego just couldn't let go.

So yes, ego is part of it. But ego does not get you through those days when you feel so defeated you just can't carry on. Imagining the looks on people's faces when they have to admit they were wrong and you were good enough does not get you past your fear of death. It takes something more. A need that pushes you past your fear. Perhaps it started out being about what the world thought of me, but it evolved into something far more personal. It became about what I thought of me. I wanted to find out if I had power over myself. With each dive, each meter I learnt something new, something more about who I could be and what I actually could do. Diving has become a way to explore who I am. I want the challenges, I want to problems, I want to learn and grow!

186 meters gave me courage and taught me that I had control – not over the rest of the world, but over my mind. For the first time in my entire I life I faced my fears and won, and in that moment, anything became possible. By following my dream to be deepest I finally grew up. I healed wounds I never knew existed.

Perhaps it is not important what drives people like me to continuously push our limits. Perhaps it is enough that we do. As a society we seem to need men and women who refuse to be scared or intimidated. I know I still do. We need the illusion of explorers. Explorers give hope to the tedium of day-to-day living. They live outside normal comfort zones and show us that there is something more. They show us that we can be something more.

Even after so many years and so many bitter disappointments, I still find the concept of explorers irresistible. They seem to have a freedom that I battle to find in a world of work, paying bills and raising a family. They see the world differently - challenging the rules and the limits. For explorers, just because something hasn't been done before, doesn't mean it's impossible. They answer to no one but themselves. It is a freedom I desperately want to own.

When you have the privilege of meeting and diving with people like Nuno, Dave and Don you can't help but admire that drive and freedom, even if it is an illusion. They give us the gift of the freedom to choose our own destinies. It is up to us whether or not we use that gift. Perhaps that is why explorers are so sorely missed; without them, our lives are that much smaller, that much darker and that much more constrained.

Deep diving has been my biggest challenge and biggest gift, and I feel that I am finally able to close that chapter of my life, leaving behind the pain and disillusionment.

I spent years being angry with Nuno for not giving me the help I thought I deserved, yet he ended up giving me the biggest gift of all. I had to learn how to do it myself. I had to learn how to be responsible for myself. I can never thank him enough for that.

Dave and Don finally shattered my illusion of glory and heroes and that's OK. Who knows if I will win my own battle with my ego, perhaps it is only important that I know it exists. At the end of the day I can look in the mirror and accept who I see there, good and bad. Mistakes will never be pleasant, but I no longer need to avoid them. How can I? The only way I can learn and grow is by doing, which means I will be getting it wrong sometimes – and that is OK.

Of all the challenges and illusions that I have had to face to be deepest, the biggest change for me has been how I see my place as a woman. In order to get where I am I had no choice but compete against some of the world's strongest men and I can truly say men are aliens. I do not understand them and I do not understand their rules. I spent years trying to imitate them, to become a man and so be accepted. I gave up my personal strengths so that I could cultivate the strengths that the men around me needed to see.

What I have come to realise is that I am not a man. I don't think like one. I don't approach problems like one and I don't have the same motivations. Sounds obvious perhaps, but in today's world with women's rights and equality being such an integral part of life I think it is an important observation, because when I look around me for a role model of a woman who has succeeded as a woman, all I see are women who are clones of the men. I can't help but wonder what will happen one day when women start playing by their own rules.

My experience as a woman in a man's world has been bittersweet and I hope I don't pass on the male-dominated view of the world I inherited from my parents to my nieces. They should be able to be successful without having to warp who they are to fit the world's definition of success. It is my uniqueness, the very fact that I am different, that has enabled me to do something that has not been done before. It is the fact that I don't approach the world like everyone else, that I don't believe what everyone else does, that has enabled me to challenge the boundaries I was expected to conform to.

As for the men who dive deep, they are to be admired, but not worshipped. Without exception, they have all been incredible divers, talented, experienced, and with iron wills. They are determined to succeed, at all costs - and do. But, without exception, I have found that they have never lived up to my expectations of who they should be as people, especially not as the heroes I made them out to be.

I am not sure if I find the destruction of this illusion to be reassuring or disturbing. These days I know that perfection isn't something we, as humans, are supposed to achieve. Life is about learning, learning is about making mistakes. Yet the illusion of perfection is hard to let go of.

(7) New Beginnings, New Dreams, New Lessons

Dave's dive was intense and my subsequent disillusionment with the world of technical diving heroes has brought me to a crossroads. Is this the end of my diving career? My experience at Boesmansgat on Dave's fateful dive didn't change my desire to dive deep (or not as the case may be). It did however show me how limited open circuit was. There was simply no way we would ever have been able to manage the support dives on open circuit and there was no way we would have been able to even plan the recovery at that depth on open circuit.

As a result, I have left my open circuit behind and moved on, into the world of re-breathers. In a way, it is a far more exciting world. Re-breathers have opened up a whole new world of diving and that has piqued my curiosity. On open circuit we have reached a point where diving deeper is going to be practically impossible. Nuno's success is a testament to his will power and sheer physical endurance. I have no doubt that men will get deeper on open circuit, using sheer will power and endurance, yet it seems to me that the true challenge in diving deep isn't for a select few to participate based on their uniqueness, but to find techniques and equipment that opens it up to the masses (so to speak). Instead of diving hard, dive smart.

I will never be able to justify the amount of will power and physical endurance that would be required to dive 300 meters and beyond, dives that take all of 12 hours. Yet the idea of exploring that deep on a machine is infinitively appealing. This is cutting edge stuff. This is true exploration in its pure sense, doing something that no other person has done before. This is new! We don't even know the questions to be asking and once we find them out, we have to create answers and that is what excites me. I love problem solving, twisting the world sideways to create new realities and new possibilities. I love creating answers, finding new ways of doing things or making the impossible possible.

It will take a while. My nieces need to get older before I can start to place my life in jeopardy. Until then I am just enjoying the gift of life. Enjoying the gift that diving has given me. I am no longer the frightened child who started diving. Instead, when I look in the mirror I see some one different. Someone more confident. More capable. I have found myself.

When I look at my journey it seems as if I have moved from the dark to the light. I have let go of the demons I inherited from my parents. More than anything my journey has been spiritual, which is hard for someone with such a strong anathema toward formal religion to admit to.

I no longer feel alone, rather instead feeling connected to a life force, call that God for want of a better word. My mother always used to tell me that I was lucky, that things always turned out for the best, and looking back, I can see that she was right.

Will I ever become the person I aspire to be? Will I ever be able to let go of the hold heroes and explorers seem to have on my definition of the world? Will I ever be able to forgive the world for letting me down, not being what I demanded? I don't know. Perhaps it isn't so important to reach your goals as to start the journey toward them.

The only limitations that exist
are the ones I believe in.

Who knows what tomorrow will bring? Perhaps I will die trying to take my machine to 300 meters; perhaps I will never make it back and see 250. Nevertheless, when I die, as I know I will, I will be able to look back on my life and see, well, a life lived. The only thing I have of value is my life. The only day I have is this one. If I die tonight I want to be at peace. Knowing I lived as hard as I could, I loved openly and without reserve and I didn't give up and fade away in fear.

The End?

You would have thought that if anyone had answers it would be I, yet I still can't answer the basic questions. Why do we dive so deep? Why do any of us aspire to be better than the rest? Are we trying to create a façade behind which we can hide? A façade of something grander then who we are? Once obtained, does this absolve us of having to do the real work, of becoming better human beings with stronger ethics and values? Do we do this for ego, so that we can bask in the admiration of others?

I have watched people claim to not be out for the 'glory' and fame that diving deep gives them. I have chosen to believe them only to discover that it was a more elaborate illusion and that after all, the drive for external recognition, worship and power is what drives them, just like the rest of us.

Us! Am I like these men? Am I this selfish, this driven by the pursuit of admiration and power of others? It petrifies me that I am also so blind, that I am like these men in more than my diving. Is my ego as strong, as selfish, as damaging to the world around me?

Perhaps aspiring to be the best person I can be is a trait that comes more closely with being a woman. I find that the record I hold is a heavy responsibility. I am no longer able to live within the quietly comfortable reality of a victim - where I don't have to take responsibility for my own destiny. Thanks to diving I know all too well that the life I live is the result of the actions I take. I am now conscious of who I am, of the consequences of my actions and so, the old ways, motivated by bitterness and personal gain are less appealing, more embarrassing.

Is it possible to be competitive in today's world without resorting to ego driven values, ethics and motivation? This journey may have started out about a record, glory and ego. These days it is more about finding out who I am and who I want to be.

Diving is just the story in which I found myself.

Appendices

Glossary

For those of you who don't know much about diving, rather than explain words and concepts in the story and bog things down, I have created a glossary of terms, names and places for quick reference.

Air	The stuff you breathe normally on the surface. Air is only one of the gases that a diver may breathe. Made up of 79% nitrogen and 21% oxygen.

Badgat	Local dive site. This is a flooded asbestos mine that has created the perfect technical dive site, providing a series of flooded passages at various depths. The deepest dive recorded here was by Dave Shaw and Don Shirley at 186 meters.
BC (Buoyancy Compensator)	This is one of the key pieces of equipment that ensures that no matter what your depth, you are always neutrally buoyant in the water. It is inflated from your cylinder.
CMAS	International diving organisation that trains and qualifies divers. French based.
DAN (Divers Alert Network)	International organisation that provides medical assistance specifically for divers. They are the key providers of recompression chambers in South Africa and manage most decompression problems experienced by divers.

Decompression Sickness (DCS)	The formation of bubbles in a diver's tissues and or blood, usually resulting from ascending too quickly. Can cause pain, paralysis heart attacks and death. This is most commonly called the bends.
Decompression/ Decompression Stop	Decompression is the process of stopping at predetermined depths on a diver's return to the surface after a deep dive. This allows any absorbed gases such as nitrogen and helium to be released from your body without causing complications or decompression sickness.
Dry Suit	A special type of diving suit that prevents water from reaching the body.
DV (Demand Valve) / Regulator	Essential piece of diving equipment that allows one to breathe underwater. This is the mechanism that transports the air stored in the dive cylinder to the diver.

END (Equivalent Narcotic Depth) / EAD (Equivalent Air Depth)	This is a standard diving term that indicates what the narcotic depth of a gas mixture would be if the mixture was in fact pure air and had no helium added to it. The industry standard is that narcotic depths should not exceed 40 meters so as to ensure the diver has full control of his mental faculties.
Gas	The stuff that a diver breathes. Your gas may be normal air or a mixture such as Heliair or Trimix.
Heliair	A gas mixture that reduces nitrogen content by simply adding helium and then normal air. The result is that both the nitrogen and oxygen content are reduced.
HPNS (High Pressure Nervous Syndrome)	A symptom that is experienced anywhere from 150 meters. The diver experiences anything from mild shaking of the hands to body convulsions. It is caused by high concentrations of helium in the mixture that is being breathed.

IANTD (International Association of Nitrox and Technical Divers)	International diving organisation that trains and qualifies technical divers.
ICD (Isobaric Counter Diffusion)	Also known as ICDS. This is a symptom experienced by divers when diving on multiple gas mixtures. The simple explanation is that instead of helium coming out of the inner ear, nitrogen is absorbed into the ear displacing the helium as bubbles. These bubbles cause vertigo, nausea and brain damage.
Narcosis or 'the narcs' (Nitrogen Narcosis)	This is the effect that nitrogen has on a diver's brain. It is like diving drunk and therefore severely affects a diver's ability to think and act under water.
NAUI	International diving training organisation, focusing on providing sport diving training.
Nitrogen	Is the major component in the air we breathe.

One star	Equivalent to Open Water One, the entry level diving qualification.
Open circuit	The familiar way of diving, with a cylinder and dv. Open circuit is characterised by the release of bubbles into the water when you breathe out.
PADI	Similar to NAUI, this is an international diving training organisation providing sport training.
PFO (Patent Foramina Ovale)	This is physical condition that is found in approximately 30% of the population. It is a hole in the heart that allows bubbles to move from one side of the heart to the other bypassing the lungs and allowing them to be released back into the main blood stream. These bubbles can lodge in the brain and or spinal cord, causing strokes and death.
Re-breather/ machine	A machine that enables a diver to reuse air by adding oxygen and removing carbon dioxide.

SAUU (South African Underwater Union)	The forerunner of CMAS in South Africa and controlling body for local dive qualifications.
SMB (Surface Marker Buoy)	An inflatable brightly coloured tube that is inflated underwater as a visual reference point for people on the surface.
Sorb	Chemical used in re-breathers to remove carbon dioxide from the exhaled breath.
TDI	International diving organisation that trains and qualifies divers. American based.
Trimix	A combination of helium, oxygen and normal air (including nitrogen) used in dives below 40 meters. The helium reduces the percentage of nitrogen and reduces risk of severe narcosis.
Vis (visibility)	Visibility under water.

Wings (type of BC)	A specific type of bc that removes need for divers to carry all their buoyancy at chest level. Specifically used by technical divers as it allows the attachment of equipment such as dive reels and torches.
WUC (Wits Underwater Club)	One of the local CMAS dive clubs that provides sport and technical dive training to students and non-students.

History of Technical Dives

Date	Event	Location	Who
1961	World Record - 220 meters.	*Switzerland*	*Keller*
1981	First recorded discovery of Boesmansgat as a dive site.	*Boesmansgat*	*Unknown*
1988	World Record, 238 meters.	*Mante, Mexico*	*Sheck Exley*
1991	Start of the first technical dive agency, IANTD. Badplaas (local dive site) discovered for diving.	*USA.* *South Africa, Badgat.*	*Unknown* *Unknown*
1993	World Record – 263 meters.	*Boesmansgat*	*Sheck Exley*
1994	Sheck Exley dies attempting to bottom Zacaton. World Record – Men 281.9 meters. Women's world record – 167 meters.	*Zacaton, Mexico* *Zacaton, Mexico* *Zacaton, Mexico*	*Sheck Exley* *Jim Bowden* *Dr Kristovich*
1994	South African Record – 230 meters. South African Record – 252 meters.	*Boesmansgat*	*Nuno Gomes*
1994	First Fatality at Boesmansgat.	*Boesmansgat*	*Deon Dryer*

Date	Event	Location	Who
1996	South African Record – 282.6 meters. World Record – Women 167 meters.	*Boesmansgat* *Zacaton, Mexico*	*Nuno Gomes* *Dr Kristovich*
2000	1st exploration of the Incline Shaft.	*Badgat*	*Verna van Schaik/ Gilbert Gunn*
2000	World Record – Women 211 meters.	*Ocean off Italy*	*Claudia Serpierri*
2001	World Record – Sea 308 meters.	*Philippines*	*John Bennett*
2001	World Record – Cave/ Altitude 186 meters.	*Boesmansgat, South Africa*	*Verna van Schaik*

Date	Event	Location	Who
2004	World Record – Women 221 meters.	Boesmansgat, South Africa	Verna van Schaik
2004	World Record – Re-breather 260 meters.	Boesmansgat, South Africa	Dave Shaw
2005	Attempted World Record – Deepest Body Recover – 260 meters.	Boesmansgat, South Africa	Dave Shaw
2005	World Record – All time, 321.8 meters.	Dahab, Red Sea	Nuno Gomes

Dive Plans

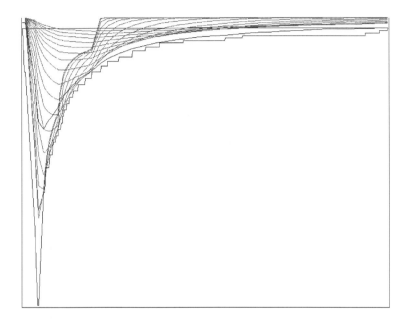

Graph 1 : *Helium Tissue Profile for 220 meter World Record Dive*

The helium tissues started to outgas from 150m (as soon from the base of the bell curve in graph 1). The first deep stop is at 130 meters, second at 100 meters. Without these (and subsequent) stops, the diver crosses over the helium tissues which indicates a high percentage of silent bubbling. These 'silent' bubbles would create an unacceptable decompression risk. My goal when creating a decompression profile is to keep the diver line away from the tissues at all times, preferably with a gap so that I never ever 'touch' an out gassing tissue.

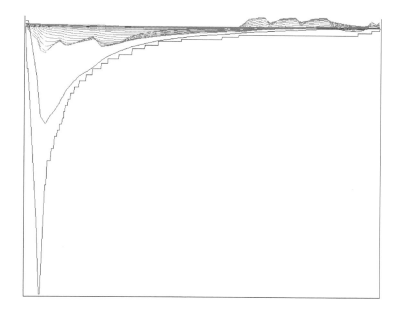

Graph 2 : *Nitrogen Tissue Profile for 220 meter World Record Dive*

DECOMPRESSION PROFILE FOR 220 m

Please note that the profile attached below was designed for a very specific dive and a specific diver and should not be re-used verbatim. There are simply no guarantees that using this profile will work in your environment or for your physiology. You do so at your own risk. Air breaks are taken for 5 minutes every 15 minutes when on pure oxygen.

Dive Summary.

Total Dive Time - 339 minutes. Total CNS - 142.6. Total OTU's - 410. Total volume gas required (no reserve included) - 29,374 litres. Altitude - 1550 meters

Stop Depth (meters)	Time (minutes)	Gas
220m	Arrive on 15 minutes	
130	6	MIX : 18:60
110	4	*(EAD 44 meters*
100	3	*ppO_2 of 1.6 bar)*
90	3	
85	3	
80	1	
75	2	
70	2	
65	3	Interim Mix 18:49
60	3	*(EAD from 12 to 28 meters*
55	4	*ppO_2 of 1.59 bar)*
50	5	
45	7	
40	7	

Stop Depth (meters)	Time (minutes)	Gas
35	9	EAN 36 *(EAD from 9 to 27 meters* *ppO₂ of 1.57 bar)*
30	7	
16	10	
23	12	
20	21	EAN 50 *(EAD from 17 to 12 meters* *ppO₂ of 1.58 bar)*
18	13	
15	13	
12	22	
10	29	
8	16	
6	115	Oxygen (25 min oxygen: 5 min air)
4	13	
2	7	

Made in the USA
Lexington, KY
17 September 2012